THE ESSENTIALS OF GREEK GRAMMAR

Oklahoma Series in Classical Culture

Oklahoma Series in Classical Culture

SERIES EDITOR

Ellen Greene, *University of Oklahoma*

ADVISORY BOARD

The Essentials of Greek Grammar

A Reference for Intermediate Readers of Attic Greek

Louise Pratt

University of Oklahoma Press : Norman

Library of Congress Cataloging-in-Publication Data

Pratt, Louise H., 1960–
   The essentials of Greek grammar : a reference for intermediate readers of Attic Greek /
Louise Pratt.
      p. cm. — (Oklahoma series in classical culture ; 39)
      ISBN 978-0-8061-4143-5 (pbk. : alk. paper)   1. Greek language—Grammar.   I. Title.

   PA258.P77   2010
   485—dc22
                                                                    2010020147

The Essentials of Greek Grammar: A Reference for Intermediate Readers of Attic Greek is Volume
39 in the Oklahoma Series in Classical Culture.

The paper in this book meets the guidelines for permanence and durability of the Committee
on Production Guidelines for Book Longevity of the Council on Library Resources, Inc. ∞

CONTENTS

Detailed Contents

Verbal adjectives

Relative clauses

Verbs: Finite

Mood: indicative, imperative, subjunctive, optative
Indicative mood

Imperative mood

Subjunctive mood
Subjunctive mood: three common independent uses

Subjunctive mood: two additional independent uses

Other

Preface and Acknowledgments

The primary purpose of this volume is to give, in a reasonably compact and accessible format, the most essential grammar needed to read texts in Attic Greek, material taught in most first-year courses in ancient Greek. This text is to serve as a reminder of that material in a format intended to help intermediate readers master it. First-year students who used an inductive reading-based textbook particularly will appreciate and profit from the outline format provided here.

This reference does not cover every grammatical point of Attic Greek, only its most common features. Students wanting a fuller account will have to turn to one of the standard Greek grammars, such as H. W. Smyth's *Greek Grammar* (2nd ed. rev. by G. M. Messing; Cambridge: Harvard University Press, 1956). This book also does not seek to teach grammar to beginners; for more detailed information at a beginning level, students will need to go back to their first-year textbooks.

This book originated in handouts distributed to students to serve as checklists for review of material taught in first year. This final version is specifically designed to support my textbook for second-year Greek: *Eros at the Banquet: Reviewing Greek with Plato's Symposium* (Norman: University of Oklahoma Press, 2011)—hence, the large number of examples drawn from the *Symposium*—but I hope that people teaching other courses will find the book useful as a reference as well, either as a review at the end of first-year Greek or as a reference for intermediate students. I have now used versions of this material with groups of students who learned Greek from the Joint Association of Classical Teachers' *Reading Greek* (Cambridge: Cambridge University Press, 1978), Anne H. Groton's *From Alpha to Omega* (Newburyport, Mass.: Focus, 2000), and Hardy Hansen and Gerald M. Quinn's *Greek: An Intensive Approach* (New York: Fordham University Press, 1992), as well as with individual students taught using various other textbooks and approaches, including Maurice Balme and Gilbert Lawall's *Athenaze* (Oxford: Oxford University Press, 2003) and Donald J. Mastronarde's *Introduction to Attic Greek* (Berkeley: University of California Press, 1993).

Students who have learned Greek using the *JACT Reading Greek* texts or another Greek text published outside North America should be advised that all declensions in this textbook are given in the standard American order: nominative, genitive, dative, accusative. If they are not ready to make the transition to standard American practice, they will need to use their first-year text as a reference for declensions.

I am enormously grateful to my students for the many comments and helpful suggestions for improvements they have provided over the years, as well as to the authors of all the first-year textbooks mentioned here from whose lucid explanations, examples, and strategies I have learned much. I have also profited from consulting C. A. E. Lushnig's *An Introduction to Ancient Greek* (New York: Scribner, 1975) and Alston Hurd Chase and Henry Phillips Jr.'s *A New Introduction to Greek* (rev. ed.; Cambridge: Harvard University Press, 1958). Peter Bing and Mike Lippman (who used versions of the original outline in their intermediate classes), Garth Tissol, and Debbie Fetter (who entered an early version of this volume into Braille for her son) provided helpful feedback and support, as did the wonderful readers and editors of the University of Oklahoma Press. For their hard work and patience in the final stages of the book's production, I am particularly grateful to my copyeditor, David Aiken, and my former student, Benjamin Cook. All have done a great deal to rein in my natural tendency toward inconsistency; I hope that I have managed to incorporate the majority of the useful suggestions given to me and apologize for any weaknesses that remain.

Finally, I thank the Emory College of Arts and Sciences and the Laney School of Graduate Studies of Emory University for the financial support they gave to the publication of this project and the Emory College Center for Teaching and Curriculum for assistance in the early stages of its development.

Abbreviations and Typographic Conventions

*-   Asterisk + hyphen immediately preceding a verb form (e.g., *-ἧκα) indicates that a verb occurs in that form only with a prefix. The breathing mark is included to indicate the presence or absence of the *h* sound, which affects the form the prefix takes (e.g., ἀφῆκα from ἀπο- + *-ἧκα).

boldface   Boldface type is used in the charts to highlight information of particular significance in that chart. Endings in boldface should be memorized, as these endings are found on many words. An entire word in boldface indicates an exceptional form in a declension or conjugation that is otherwise predictable. Note, however, that individual forms in irregular conjugations and declensions are not highlighted; the assumption is that the entire chart needs the same degree of attention.

[ ]   Square brackets in charts enclose uncontracted versions of endings that undergo contraction in Attic. Some of these uncontracted versions are found in other dialects and can help students see the relationship between contracted and regular forms of the endings, aiding memory.

1aor.	first aorist (also called weak aorist)
1perf.	first perfect
1st	first person
2aor.	second aorist (also called strong aorist)
2nd	second person
2perf.	second perfect
3rd	third person
abs.	absolute
acc.	accusative
act.	active
adj.	adjective
adv.	adverb

aor.	aorist
artic.	articular
aug.	augment
compar.	comparative
compl.	complement
conj.	conjunction
contr.	contracted
correl.	correlative
dat.	dative
decl.	declension
def. art.	definite article
demonst.	demonstrative
dir.	direct
fem.	feminine
fut.	future
gen.	genitive
impera.	imperative
imperf.	imperfect
impers.	impersonal, impersonally
indecl.	indeclinable
indef.	indefinite
indic.	indicative
indir.	indirect
inf.	infinitive
interrog.	interrogative
intrans.	intransitive
irreg.	irregular
masc.	masculine
mid.	middle
neut.	neuter
nom.	nominative
obj.	object, objective
opt.	optative
part.	participle
pass.	passive
perf.	perfect
pers.	person
pl.	plural
pluperf.	pluperfect
pred.	predicate

prep.	preposition
pres.	present
princ. part	principal part
pron.	pronoun
refl.	reflexive
reg.	regular
rel.	relative
sing.	singular
subje.	subject, subjective
subju.	subjunctive
subst.	substantive
superl.	superlative
suppl.	supplemental
trans.	transitive
voc.	vocative

Part 1
Forms

Article and Pronouns

§ 1 Definite article

	masc.	fem.	neut.
nom. sing.	ὁ	ἡ	τό
gen. sing.	τοῦ	τῆς	τοῦ
dat. sing.	τῷ	τῇ	τῷ
acc. sing.	τόν	τήν	τό
nom. pl.	οἱ	αἱ	τά
gen. pl.	τῶν	τῶν	τῶν
dat. pl.	τοῖς	ταῖς	τοῖς
acc. pl.	τούς	τάς	τά

§ 2 Personal pronouns

	1st sing. ("I, me")	2nd sing. ("you")	3rd sing. ("him, her, it")*
nom. sing.	ἐγώ	σύ	—
gen. sing.	ἐμοῦ/μου	σοῦ/σου	οὗ
dat. sing.	ἐμοί/μοι	σοί/σοι	οἷ
acc. sing.	ἐμέ/με	σέ/σε	ἕ
	1st pl. ("we, us")	**2nd pl. ("you")**	**3rd pl. ("they, them")***
nom. pl.	ἡμεῖς	ὑμεῖς	σφεῖς
gen. pl.	ἡμῶν	ὑμῶν	σφῶν
dat. pl.	ἡμῖν	ὑμῖν	σφίσι(ν)
acc. pl.	ἡμᾶς	ὑμᾶς	σφᾶς

*Rare in Attic prose, where demonstratives (οὗτος, ἐκεῖνος, ὅδε) or oblique (non-nominative) cases of αὐτός are used instead.

§ **3** **αὐτός -ή -ό** (*singular* him, her, it, ——self; *plural* them, ——selves) (§§200–205)

	masc.	fem.	neut.
nom. sing.	αὐτός	αὐτή	αὐτό
gen. sing.	αὐτοῦ	αὐτῆς	αὐτοῦ
dat. sing.	αὐτῷ	αὐτῇ	αὐτῷ
acc. sing.	αὐτόν	αὐτήν	αὐτό
nom. pl.	αὐτοί	αὐταί	αὐτά
gen. pl.	αὐτῶν	αὐτῶν	αὐτῶν
dat. pl.	αὐτοῖς	αὐταῖς	αὐτοῖς
acc. pl.	αὐτούς	αὐτάς	αὐτά

§ **4** **ὅς ἥ ὅ** (who, which, that, etc.): relative pronoun (§§129–135)

	masc.	fem.	neut.
nom. sing.	ὅς	ἥ	ὅ
gen. sing.	οὗ	ἧς	οὗ
dat. sing.	ᾧ	ᾗ	ᾧ
acc. sing.	ὅν	ἥν	ὅ
nom. pl.	οἵ	αἵ	ἅ
gen. pl.	ὧν	ὧν	ὧν
dat. pl.	οἷς	αἷς	οἷς
acc. pl.	οὕς	ἅς	ἅ

§ **5** **ὅστις ἥτις ὅ τι/ὅτι** (who[ever], someone/anyone who, which[ever], something/anything which, etc.): indefinite relative pronoun (§§129–135)

	masc.	fem.	neut.
nom. sing.	ὅστις	ἥτις	ὅ τι/ὅτι (**in Plato**)
gen. sing.	οὗτινος/ὅτου	ἧστινος	οὗτινος/ὅτου
dat. sing.	ᾧτινι/ὅτῳ	ᾗτινι	ᾧτινι/ὅτῳ
acc. sing.	ὅντινα	ἥντινα	ὅ τι/ὅτι (**in Plato**)
nom. pl.	οἵτινες	αἵτινες	ἅτινα/ἅττα
gen. pl.	ὧντινων/ὅτων	ὧντινων	ὧντινων/ὅτων
dat. pl.	οἷστισι(ν)/ὅτοις	αἷστισι(ν)	οἷστισι(ν)/ὅτοις
acc. pl.	οὕστινας	ἅστινας	ἅτινα/ἅττα

Adjectives

§ 6 First/second declension adjective (nominative endings: -ος -η -ον)

	masc.	fem.	neut.
nom. sing.	καλός	καλή	καλόν
gen. sing.	καλοῦ	καλῆς	καλοῦ
dat. sing.	καλῷ	καλῇ	καλῷ
acc. sing.	καλόν	καλήν	καλόν
nom. pl.	καλοί	καλαί	καλά
gen. pl.	καλῶν	καλῶν	καλῶν
dat. pl.	καλοῖς	καλαῖς	καλοῖς
acc. pl.	καλούς	καλάς	καλά

§ 7 First/second declension adjective (nominative endings: -ος -α -ον)

	masc.	fem.	neut.
nom. sing.	ἄθλιος	ἀθλία	ἄθλιον
gen. sing.	ἀθλίου	ἀθλίας	ἀθλίου
dat. sing.	ἀθλίῳ	ἀθλίᾳ	ἀθλίῳ
acc. sing.	ἄθλιον	ἀθλίαν	ἄθλιον
nom. pl.	ἄθλιοι	ἄθλιαι	ἄθλια
gen. pl.	ἀθλίων	ἀθλίων	ἀθλίων
dat. pl.	ἀθλίοις	ἀθλίαις	ἀθλίοις
acc. pl.	ἀθλίους	ἀθλίας	ἄθλια

§ 8 Two-termination second declension adjective (nominative endings: -ος -ον)

	masc./fem.	neut.
nom. sing.	ἄδηλος	ἄδηλον
gen. sing.	ἀδήλου	ἀδήλου
dat. sing.	ἀδήλῳ	ἀδήλῳ
acc. sing.	ἄδηλον	ἄδηλον
nom. pl.	ἄδηλοι	ἄδηλα
gen. pl.	ἀδήλων	ἀδήλων
dat. pl.	ἀδήλοις	ἀδήλοις
acc. pl.	ἀδήλους	ἄδηλα

§ 9 πολύς πολλή πολύ (*singular* much; *plural* many): irregular first/second declension adjective (cf. §3, §13)

	masc.	fem.	neut.
nom. sing.	**πολύς**	πολλή	**πολύ**
gen. sing.	πολλοῦ	πολλῆς	πολλοῦ
dat. sing.	πολλῷ	πολλῇ	πολλῷ
acc. sing.	**πολύν**	πολλήν	**πολύ**
nom. pl.	πολλοί	πολλαί	πολλά
gen. pl.	πολλῶν	πολλῶν	πολλῶν
dat. pl.	πολλοῖς	πολλαῖς	πολλοῖς
acc. pl.	πολλούς	πολλάς	πολλά

§ 10 μέγας μεγάλη μέγα (great, big): irregular first/second declension adjective

	masc.	fem.	neut.
nom. sing.	**μέγας**	μεγάλη	**μέγα**
gen. sing.	μεγάλου	μεγάλης	μεγάλου
dat. sing.	μεγάλῳ	μεγάλῃ	μεγάλῳ
acc. sing.	**μέγαν**	μεγάλην	**μέγα**
nom. pl.	μεγάλοι	μεγάλαι	μεγάλα
gen. pl.	μεγάλων	μεγάλων	μεγάλων
dat. pl.	μεγάλοις	μεγάλαις	μεγάλοις
acc. pl.	μεγάλους	μεγάλας	μεγάλα

§ 11 οὗτος αὕτη τοῦτο (*singular* this; *plural* these): demonstrative adjective (cf. §3, §9, §13)

	masc.	fem.	neut.
nom. sing.	οὗτος	αὕτη	τοῦτο
gen. sing.	τούτου	ταύτης	τούτου
dat. sing.	τούτῳ	ταύτῃ	τούτῳ
acc. sing.	τοῦτον	ταύτην	τοῦτο
nom. pl.	οὗτοι	αὗται	ταῦτα
gen. pl.	τούτων	τούτων	τούτων
dat. pl.	τούτοις	ταύταις	τούτοις
acc. pl.	τούτους	ταύτας	ταῦτα

§ 12 ἐκεῖνος ἐκείνη ἐκεῖνο (*singular* that; *plural* those): demonstrative adjective (cf. §3, §9, §11, §13)

	masc.	fem.	neut.
nom. sing.	ἐκεῖνος	ἐκείνη	**ἐκεῖνο**
gen. sing.	ἐκείνου	ἐκείνης	ἐκείνου
dat. sing.	ἐκείνῳ	ἐκείνῃ	ἐκείνῳ
acc. sing.	ἐκεῖνον	ἐκείνην	**ἐκεῖνο**
nom. pl.	ἐκεῖνοι	ἐκεῖναι	ἐκεῖνα
gen. pl.	ἐκείνων	ἐκείνων	ἐκείνων
dat. pl.	ἐκείνοις	ἐκείναις	ἐκείνοις
acc. pl.	ἐκείνους	ἐκείνας	ἐκεῖνα

§ 13 ὅδε ἥδε τόδε (*singular* this [here], this [following]; *plural* these [here], these [following]): demonstrative adjective

	masc.	fem.	neut.
nom. sing.	ὅδε	ἥδε	τόδε
gen. sing.	τοῦδε	τῆσδε	τοῦδε
dat. sing.	τῷδε	τῇδε	τῷδε
acc. sing.	τόνδε	τήνδε	τόδε
nom. pl.	οἵδε	αἵδε	τάδε
gen. pl.	τῶνδε	τῶνδε	τῶνδε
dat. pl.	τοῖσδε	ταῖσδε	τοῖσδε
acc. pl.	τούσδε	τάσδε	τάδε

§ 14 Regular third declension adjective (nominative endings: -ων -ον)

	masc./fem.	neut.
nom. sing.	κακοδαίμων	κακόδαιμον
gen. sing.	κακοδαίμονος	κακοδαίμονος
dat. sing.	κακοδαίμονι	κακοδαίμονι
acc. sing.	κακοδαίμονα	κακόδαιμον
nom. pl.	κακοδαίμονες	κακοδαίμονα
gen. pl.	κακοδαιμόνων	κακοδαιμόνων
dat. pl.	κακοδαίμοσι(ν)	κακοδαίμοσι(ν)
acc. pl.	κακοδαίμονας	κακοδαίμονα

§ 15 τίς τί (τιν-): interrogative pronoun/adjective (third declension)

	masc./fem.	neut.
	who? what *noun*? which *noun*?	what? why? what *noun*? which *noun*?
nom. sing.	τίς	τί
gen. sing.	τίνος	τίνος
dat. sing.	τίνι	τίνι
acc. sing.	τίνα	τί
nom. pl.	τίνες	τίνα
gen. pl.	τίνων	τίνων
dat. pl.	τίσι(ν)	τίσι(ν)
acc. pl.	τίνας	τίνα

§ 16 τις τι (τιν-): indefinite pronoun/adjective (third declension)

	masc./fem.	neut.
	someone, anyone, a certain *noun*, a *noun*, some *noun*	something, anything, a certain *noun*, a *noun*, some *noun*
nom. sing.	τις	τι
gen. sing.	τινός/του	τινός/του
dat. sing.	τινί/τῳ	τινί/τῳ
acc. sing.	τινά	τι
nom. pl.	τινές	τινά
gen. pl.	τινῶν	τινῶν
dat. pl.	τισί(ν)	τισί(ν)
acc. pl.	τινάς	τινά

§ 17 Contracted third declension adjective (nominative endings: -ης -ες)

	masc./fem.	neut.
nom. sing.	σαφής	σαφές
gen. sing.	σαφοῦς [-έος]	σαφοῦς [-έος]
dat. sing.	σαφεῖ [-έι]	σαφεῖ [-έι]
acc. sing.	σαφῆ [-έα]	σαφές
nom. pl.	σαφεῖς [-έες]	σαφῆ [-έα]
gen. pl.	σαφῶν [-έων]	σαφῶν [-έων]
dat. pl.	σαφέσι(ν)	σαφέσι(ν)
acc. pl.	σαφεῖς	σαφῆ [-έα]

§ 18 οὐδείς οὐδεμία οὐδέν (οὐδεν-) (no one, none, no): mixed-declension adjective

	masc.	fem.	neut.
	no one, nobody, no *noun*	no woman, no *noun*	nothing, no *noun*
nom. sing.	οὐδείς	οὐδεμία	οὐδέν
gen. sing.	οὐδενός	οὐδεμᾶς	οὐδενός
dat. sing.	οὐδενί	οὐδεμιᾷ	οὐδενί
acc. sing.	οὐδένα	οὐδεμίαν	οὐδέν

§ 19 πᾶς πᾶσα πᾶν (παντ-) (all, every): mixed-declension adjective

	masc.	fem.	neut.
nom. sing.	πᾶς	πᾶσα	πᾶν
gen. sing.	παντός	πάσης	παντός
dat. sing.	παντί	πάσῃ	παντί
acc. sing.	πάντα	πᾶσαν	πᾶν
nom. pl.	πάντες	πᾶσαι	πάντα
gen. pl.	πάντων	πασῶν	πάντων
dat. pl.	πᾶσι(ν)	πάσαις	πᾶσι(ν)
acc. pl.	πάντας	πάσας	πάντα

20 Mixed-declension adjective (nominative endings: -ας -αινα -αν)

	masc.	fem.	neut.
nom. sing.	τάλας	τάλαινα	τάλαν
gen. sing.	τάλανος	ταλαίνης	τάλανος
dat. sing.	τάλανι	ταλαίνῃ	τάλανι
acc. sing.	τάλανα	τάλαιναν	τάλαν
nom. pl.	τάλανες	τάλαιναι	τάλανα
gen. pl.	ταλάνων	ταλαινῶν	ταλάνων
dat. pl.	τάλασι(ν)	ταλαίναις	τάλασι(ν)
acc. pl.	τάλανας	ταλαίνας	τάλανα

§ 21 Mixed-declension adjective (nominative endings: -υς -εια -υ)

	masc.	fem.	neut.
nom. sing.	γλυκύς	γλυκεῖα	γλυκύ
gen. sing.	γλυκέος	γλυκείας	γλυκέος
dat. sing.	γλυκεῖ	γλυκείᾳ	γλυκεῖ
acc. sing.	γλυκύν	γλυκεῖαν	γλυκύ
nom. pl.	γλυκεῖς	γλυκεῖαι	γλυκέα
gen. pl.	γλυκέων	γλυκειῶν	γλυκέων
dat. pl.	γλυκέσι(ν)	γλυκείαις	γλυκέσι(ν)
acc. pl.	γλυκεῖς	γλυκείας	γλυκέα

§ 22 Regular comparative and superlative adjectives

	compar.: most decline like ἄθλιος -α -ον (§7)	superl.: all decline like καλός -ή -όν (§6)
σοφός -ή -όν*	σοφώτερος -α -ον	σοφώτατος -η -ον
ἄθλιος -α -ον*	ἀθλιώτερος -α -ον	ἀθλιώτατος -η -ον
δεινός -ή -όν†	δεινότερος -α -ον	δεινότατος -η -ον
ἄδηλος -ον†	ἀδηλότερος -α -ον	ἀδηλότατος -η -ον
εὐδαίμων -ον (-ονος)	εὐδαιμονέστερος -α -ον	εὐδαιμονέστατος -η -ον
σαφής -ές	σαφέστερος -α -ον	σαφέστατος -η -ον
γλυκύς -εῖα -ύ	γλυκίων -ον (§24)	γλύκιστος -η -ον

* Final syllable of stem is short.
† Final syllable of stem is long.

§ 23 Irregular comparative and superlative adjectives

positive (if extant)	compar. (§24)	superl.: decline like καλός -ή -όν (§6)
ἀγαθός -ή -όν	ἀμείνων -ον	ἄριστος -η -ον
" "	βελτίων -ον	βέλτιστος -η -ον
αἰσχρός -ά -όν	αἰσχίων -ον	αἴσχιστος -η -ον
(μικρός -ά -όν)	ἐλάττων -ον	ἐλάχιστος -η -ον
ἐχθρός -ά -όν	ἐχθίων -ον	ἔχθιστος -η -ον
κακός -ή -όν	κακίων -ον	κάκιστος -η -ον
" "	χείρων -ον	χείριστος -η -ον
" "	ἥττων -ον	ἥκιστος -η -ον
καλός -ή -όν	καλλίων -ον	κάλλιστος -η -ον
—	κρείττων -ον	κράτιστος -η -ον
μέγας μεγάλη μέγα	μείζων -ον	μέγιστος -η -ον
πολύς πολλά πολύ	πλείων -ον/πλέων -ον	πλεῖστος -η -ον
ῥάδιος -α -ον	ῥάων -ον	ῥᾷστος -η -ον
ταχύς -εῖα -ύ	θάττων -ον	τάχιστος -η -ον

§ 24 Irregular comparative adjective (declension)

- very often contracted (contracted forms given in parentheses), otherwise identical to regular third declension adjective (§14)

	masc./fem.	neut.
nom. sing.	βελτίων	βέλτιον
gen. sing.	βελτίονος	βελτίονος
dat. sing.	βελτίονι	βελτίονι
acc. sing.	βελτίονα (βελτίω)	βέλτιον
nom. pl.	βελτίονες (βελτίους)	βελτίονα (βελτίω)
gen. pl.	βελτιόνων	βελτιόνων
dat. pl.	βελτίοσι(ν)	βελτίοσι(ν)
acc. pl.	βελτίονας (βελτίους)	βελτίονα (βελτίω)

Participles

§ 25 Present participle of εἰμί (being)

	masc.	fem.	neut.
nom. sing.	ὤν	οὖσα	ὄν
gen. sing.	ὄντος	οὔσης	ὄντος
dat. sing.	ὄντι	οὔσῃ	ὄντι
acc. sing.	ὄντα	οὖσαν	ὄν
nom. pl.	ὄντες	οὖσαι	ὄντα
gen. pl.	ὄντων	οὐσῶν	ὄντων
dat. pl.	οὖσι(ν)	οὔσαις	οὖσι(ν)
acc. pl.	ὄντας	οὔσας	ὄντα

§ 26 Present active participle of regular verb (e.g., λύω): "——ing"

- present stem (first principal part minus ending) + -ων -ουσα -ον
- declines like ὤν οὖσα ὄν (§25)

	masc.	fem.	neut.
nom. sing.	λύων	λύουσα	λῦον
gen. sing.	λύοντος	λυούσης	λύοντος
dat. sing.	λύοντι	λυούσῃ	λύοντι
acc. sing.	λύοντα	λύουσαν	λῦον
nom. pl.	λύοντες	λύουσαι	λύοντα
gen. pl.	λυόντων	λυουσῶν	λυόντων
dat. pl.	λύουσι(ν)	λυούσαις	λύουσι(ν)
acc. pl.	λύοντας	λυούσας	λύοντα

§ 27 Present active participles of contract verbs (e.g., ἐράω, φιλέω, δηλόω): "——ing"

- Decline essentially like present active participle of regular verbs (§26), but nominative singular forms and stems are slightly different.

	masc.	fem.	neut.
ἐράω	*nom. sing.*: ἐρῶν	*nom. sing.*: ἐρῶσα	*nom. sing.*: ἐρῶν
(alpha-contract)	*stem*: ἐρωντ-	*stem*: ἐρωσ-	*stem*: ἐρωντ-
φιλέω	*nom. sing.*: φιλῶν	*nom. sing.*: φιλοῦσα	*nom. sing.*: φιλοῦν
(epsilon-contract)	*stem*: φιλουντ-	*stem*: φιλουσ-	*stem*: φιλουντ-
δηλόω	*nom. sing.*: δηλῶν	*nom. sing.*: δηλοῦσα	*nom. sing.*: δηλοῦν
(omicron-contract)	*stem*: δηλουντ-	*stem*: δηλουσ-	*stem*: δηλουντ-

§ 28 Present active participles of -μι verbs: "——ing"

- Decline essentially like present active participle of regular verbs (§26), but nominative singular forms can look very different.

	masc.	fem.	neut.
δίδωμι	*nom. sing.*: διδούς	*nom. sing.*: διδοῦσα	*nom. sing.*: διδόν
	stem: διδοντ-	*stem*: διδουσ-	*stem*: διδοντ-
τίθημι	*nom. sing.*: τιθείς	*nom. sing.*: τιθεῖσα	*nom. sing.*: τιθέν
	stem: τιθεντ-	*stem*: τιθεισ-	*stem*: τιθεντ-
ἵστημι	*nom. sing.*: ἱστάς	*nom. sing.*: ἱστᾶσα	*nom. sing.*: ἱστάν
	stem: ἱσταντ-	*stem*: ἱστασ-	*stem*: ἱσταντ-
δείκνυμι	*nom. sing.*: δεικνύς	*nom. sing.*: δεικνῦσα	*nom. sing.*: δεικνύν
	stem: δεικνυντ-	*stem*: δεικνυσ-	*stem*: δεικνυντ-
ἵημι	*nom. sing.*: ἱείς	*nom. sing.*: ἱεῖσα	*nom. sing.*: ἱέν
	stem: ἱεντ-	*stem*: ἱεισ-	*stem*: ἱεντ-
εἶμι	*nom. sing.*: ἰών	*nom. sing.*: ἰοῦσα	*nom. sing.*: ἰόν
	stem: ἰοντ-	*stem*: ἰουσ-	*stem*: ἰοντ-

§ 29 Future active participles: "about to ——, in order to ——"

- Decline like present active participle (§26), but uses the future stem (second principal part minus ending).
- Many verbs consistently use the middle voice in the future; such verbs will, of course, have a future participle that uses middle endings (§34).
- Some verbs are epsilon-contract in the future and will use epsilon-contract forms and stems (§27).

verb	fut. indic.	masc. part. nom. sing.	fem. part. nom. sing.	neut. part. nom. sing.
λύω	λύσω	λύσων	λύσουσα	λῦσον
πέμπω	πέμψω	πέμψων	πέμψουσα	πέμψον
ἄγω	ἄξω	ἄξων	ἄξουσα	ἄξον
φιλέω	φιλήσω	φιλήσων	φιλήσουσα	φίλησον
δηλόω	δηλώσω	δηλώσων	δηλώσουσα	δήλωσον
βάλλω	βαλῶ (epsilon-contract)	βαλῶν	βαλοῦσα	βαλοῦν

§ 30 First (weak) aorist active participle: "——ing, upon ——ing, having ——ed"

- aorist active stem (third principal part minus temporal augment and ending) + -ας -ασα -αν (-αντ-)

	masc.	fem.	neut.
nom. sing.	λύσας	λύσασα	λῦσαν
gen. sing.	λύσαντος	λυσάσης	λύσαντος
dat. sing.	λύσαντι	λυσάσῃ	λύσαντι
acc. sing.	λύσαντα	λύσασαν	λῦσαν
nom. pl.	λύσαντες	λύσασαι	λύσαντα
gen. pl.	λυσάντων	λυσασῶν	λυσάντων
dat. pl.	λύσασι(ν)	λυσάσαις	λύσασι(ν)
acc. pl.	λύσαντας	λυσάσας	λύσαντα

§ 31 Second (strong) aorist active participle: "——ing, upon ——ing, having ——ed"

- second (strong) aorist active stem (third principal part minus temporal augment and ending) + -ών -οῦσα -όν (-όντ-)

	masc.	fem.	neut.
nom. sing.	λαβών	λαβοῦσα	λαβόν
gen. sing.	λαβόντος	λαβούσης	λαβόντος
dat. sing.	λαβόντι	λαβούσῃ	λαβόντι
acc. sing.	λαβόντα	λαβοῦσαν	λαβόν
nom. pl.	λαβόντες	λαβοῦσαι	λαβόντα
gen. pl.	λαβόντων	λαβουσῶν	λαβόντων
dat. pl.	λαβοῦσι(ν)	λαβούσαις	λαβοῦσι(ν)
acc. pl.	λαβόντας	λαβούσας	λαβόντα

§ 32 Aorist active participle of -μι verbs and root aorists: "——ing, upon ——ing, having ——ed"

- Follows the basic active participle declension (§26, §31), although nominative singular forms and stems vary.

	masc.	fem.	neut.
δίδωμι	*nom. sing.:* δούς	*nom. sing.:* δοῦσα	*nom. sing.:* δόν
	stem: δοντ-	*stem:* δουσ-	*stem:* δοντ-
τίθημι	*nom. sing.:* θείς	*nom. sing.:* θεῖσα	*nom. sing.:* θέν
	stem: θεντ-	*stem:* θεισ-	*stem:* θεντ-
ἵημι	*nom. sing.:* εἵς	*nom. sing.:* εῖσα	*nom. sing.:* ἕν
	stem: ἑντ-	*stem:* εἱσ-	*stem:* ἑντ-
ἵστημι (root aor.)	*nom. sing.:* στάς	*nom. sing.:* στᾶσα	*nom. sing.:* στάν
	stem: σταντ-	*stem:* στασ-	*stem:* σταντ-
βαίνω (root aor.)	*nom. sing.:* βάς	*nom. sing.:* βᾶσα	*nom. sing.:* βάν
	stem: βαντ-	*stem:* βασ-	*stem:* βαντ-
γιγνώσκω (root aor.)	*nom. sing.:* γνούς	*nom. sing.:* γνοῦσα	*nom. sing.:* γνόν
	stem: γνοντ-	*stem:* γνουσ-	*stem:* γνοντ-

§ 33 Perfect active participle: "having ——ed"

- perfect active stem (fourth principal part minus ending) + -ώς -υῖα -ός

	masc.	fem.	neut.
nom. sing.	λελυκώς	λελυκυῖα	λελυκός
gen. sing.	λελυκότος	λελυκυίας	λελυκότος
dat. sing.	λελυκότι	λελυκυίᾳ	λελυκότι
acc. sing.	λελυκότα	λελυκυῖαν	λελυκός
nom. pl.	λελυκότες	λελυκυῖαι	λελυκότα
gen. pl.	λελυκότων	λελυκυιῶν	λελυκότων
dat. pl.	λελυκόσι(ν)	λελυκυίαις	λελυκόσι(ν)
acc. pl.	λελυκότας	λελυκυίας	λελυκότα

§ 34 Present middle-passive participle of regular verb: *middle* "——ing, ——ing [oneself]"; *passive* "being ——ed, ——ed"

- present stem (first principal part minus ending) + -όμενος -ομένη -όμενον
- declines like regular first/second declension adjective (§6)

	masc.	fem.	neut.
nom. sing.	λυόμενος	λυομένη	λυόμενον
gen. sing.	λυομένου	λυομένης	λυομένου
dat. sing.	λυομένῳ	λυομένῃ	λυομένῳ
acc. sing.	λυόμενον	λυομένην	λυόμενον
nom. pl.	λυόμενοι	λυόμεναι	λυόμενα
gen. pl.	λυομένων	λυομένων	λυομένων
dat. pl.	λυομένοις	λυομέναις	λυομένοις
acc. pl.	λυομένους	λυομένας	λυόμενα

§ 35 Present middle-passive participles of contract and -μι verbs: *middle* "——ing, ——ing [oneself]"; *passive* "being ——ed, ——ed"

- decline like regular present middle-passive participle (§34), with only slight differences in stem

	masc. nom. sing.	fem. nom. sing.	neut. nom. sing.
ἐράω (alpha-contract)	ἐρώμενος	ἐρωμένη	ἐρώμενον
φιλέω (epsilon-contract)	φιλούμενος	φιλουμένη	φιλούμενον
δηλόω (omicron-contract)	δηλούμενος	δηλουμένη	δηλούμενον
δίδωμι	διδόμενος	διδομένη	διδόμενον
τίθημι	τιθέμενος	τιθεμένη	τιθέμενον
ἵστημι	ἱστάμενος	ἱσταμένη	ἱστάμενον
δείκνυμι	δεικνύμενος	δεικνυμένη	δεικνύμενον
ἵημι	ἱέμενος	ἱεμένη	ἱέμενον

§ 36 Future middle and passive participles: *middle* "about to be ——ing, going to ——, in order to —— [oneself, for oneself]," etc.; *passive* "about to be ——ed, going to be ——ed, in order to be ——ed," etc.

- decline like regular middle-passive participle (§34) but use different stems
- future middle participle: future stem (second principal part minus ending) + -όμενος -ομένη -όμενον
- future passive participle: aorist passive stem (sixth principal part minus temporal augment and ending) + -ησόμενος -ησομένη -ησόμενον

§ 37 Aorist middle participles: "upon ——ing, having ——ed, ——ing [oneself, for oneself]," etc.

- decline like present middle-passive participle (§34) but use different stems
- first/weak aorist middle participle: aorist stem (third principal part minus temporal augment and ending) + -άμενος -αμένη -άμενον
- second/strong aorist middle participle: aorist stem (third principal part minus temporal augment and ending) + -όμενος -ομένη -όμενον
- for stems of athematic (-μι) verbs, see chart below

	masc. nom. sing.	fem. nom. sing.	neut. nom. sing.
δίδωμι	δόμενος	δομένη	δόμενον
τίθημι	θέμενος	θεμένη	θέμενον
ἵστημι	στάμενος	σταμένη	στάμενον
δείκνυμι*	δειξάμενος	δειξαμένη	δειξάμενον
ἵημι	*-έμενος	*-έμένη	*-έμενον

*Δείκνυμι has a regular first (weak) aorist.

§ 38 Aorist passive participle: "upon being ——ed, having been ——ed, ——ed," etc.

- follows the basic declension pattern of active participles (§26, §30, §31, §33)
- aorist passive stem (sixth principal part minus temporal augment and ending) + -είς -εῖσα -έν

	masc.	fem.	neut.
nom. sing.	λυθείς	λυθεῖσα	λυθέν
gen. sing.	λυθέντος	λυθείσης	λυθέντος
dat. sing.	λυθέντι	λυθείσῃ	λυθέντι
acc. sing.	λυθέντα	λυθεῖσαν	λυθέν
nom. pl.	λυθέντες	λυθεῖσαι	λυθέντα
gen. pl.	λυθέντων	λυθεισῶν	λυθέντων
dat. pl.	λυθεῖσι(ν)	λυθείσαις	λυθεῖσι(ν)
acc. pl.	λυθέντας	λυθείσας	λυθέντα

§ 39 Summary of middle-passive participles of a regular verb (e.g., λύω)

- Apart from aorist passive (§38), all middle and passive participles follow essentially the same declension as present middle participle (§34), but use different stems, as appropriate (§§35–37).

- The perfect middle-passive participle uses the perfect middle-passive stem (fifth principal part minus ending) + -μένος -μένη -μένον.

	masc. nom. sing.	fem. nom. sing.	neut. nom. sing.
pres. mid.-pass.	λυόμενος	λυομένη	λυόμενον
fut. mid.	λυσόμενος	λυσομένη	λυσόμενον
fut. pass.	λυθησόμενος	λυθησομένη	λυθησόμενον
aor. mid.	λυσάμενος	λυσαμένη	λυσάμενον
aor. pass.	λυθείς	λυθεῖσα	λυθέν
perf. mid.-pass.	λελυμένος	λελυμένη	λελυμένον

§ 40 Summary of middle-passive participles of a verb with variant principal parts (e.g., λαμβάνω λήψομαι ἔλαβον εἴληφα εἴλημμαι ἐλήφθην)

- Apart from aorist passive (§38), all middle and passive participles follow essentially the same declension as present middle participle (§34), but use different stems, as appropriate (§§35–37).

- The perfect middle-passive participle uses the perfect middle-passive stem (fifth principal part minus ending) + -μένος -μένη -μένον.

	masc. nom. sing.	fem. nom. sing.	neut. nom. sing.
pres. mid.-pass.	λαμβανόμενος	λαμβανομένη	λαμβανόμενον
fut. mid.	ληψόμενος	ληψομένη	ληψόμενον
fut. pass.	ληφθησόμενος	ληφθησομένη	ληφθησόμενον
aor. mid.	λαβόμενος	λαβομένη	λαβόμενον
aor. pass.	ληφθείς	ληφθεῖσα	ληφθέν
perf. mid.-pass.	εἰλημμένος	εἰλημμένη	εἰλημμένον

Nouns

§ 41 Summary of noun endings

The letters that follow the number of the declension (e.g., 1a, 2b) are used to distinguish variant types within the same basic declension. They are nearly identical to those used by the Joint Association of Classical Teachers in the Reading Greek series (but 3c and 3d are reversed and 1e is an innovation).

	1st decl.					2nd decl.		3rd decl. (consonant stem)	
	fem.			masc.		masc./fem.	neut.	masc./fem.	neut.
	1a	1b	1c	1d	1e	2a	2b	3a	3b
nom. sing.	-η	-α	-α	-ης	-ας	-ος	-ον	—	—
gen. sing.	-ης	-ας	-ης	-ου	-ου	-ου	-ου	-ος	-ος
dat. sing.	-ῃ	-ᾳ	-ῃ	-ῃ	-ᾳ	-ῳ	-ῳ	-ι	-ι
acc. sing.	-ην	-αν	-αν	-ην	-αν	-ον	-ον	-α	—
nom. pl.	-αι	-αι	-αι	-αι	-αι	-οι	-α	-ες	-α
gen. pl.	-ῶν	-ῶν	-ῶν	-ῶν	-ῶν	-ων	-ων	-ων	-ων
dat. pl.	-αις	-αις	-αις	-αις	-αις	-οις	-οις	-σι(ν)*	-σι(ν)*
acc. pl.	-ας	-ας	-ας	-ας	-ας	-ους	-α	-ας	-α

*Dative plural of third declension: in the third declension, when the consonant of the stem meets the -σι of the dative plural ending, these forms result (with some exceptions):

$$\begin{aligned} &\pi, \beta, \varphi + \text{-}\sigma\iota = \text{-}\psi\iota & \nu + \text{-}\sigma\iota = \text{-}\sigma\iota & \varrho + \text{-}\sigma\iota = \text{-}\varrho\sigma\iota \\ &\varkappa, \gamma, \chi + \text{-}\sigma\iota = \text{-}\xi\iota & \sigma + \text{-}\sigma\iota = \text{-}\sigma\iota & \lambda + \text{-}\sigma\iota = \text{-}\lambda\sigma\iota \\ & & \tau, \delta, \theta + \text{-}\sigma\iota = \text{-}\sigma\iota \end{aligned}$$

3rd decl. (continued)

	masc./fem.	neut.	masc./fem.	neut.	masc./fem.	
	3c	**3d**	**3e**	**3f**	**3g**	**3h**
nom. sing.	-ης	-ος	-ις/-υς	-υ	-εύς	-υς
gen. sing.	-ους [-εος]	-ους [-εος]	-εως	-εως	-έως	-υος
dat. sing.	-ει	-ει	-ει	-ει	-εῖ	-υι
acc. sing.	-η [-εα]	-ος	-ιν/-υν	-υ	-έα	-υν
nom. pl.	-εις [-εες]	-η [-εα]	-εις	-η [-εα]	-εῖς/-ῆς	-υες
gen. pl.	-ῶν [-έων]	-ῶν [-έων]	-εων	-εων	-έων	-ύων
dat. pl.	-εσι(ν)	-εσι(ν)	-εσι(ν)	-εσι(ν)	-εῦσι(ν)	-υσι(ν)
acc. pl.	-εις	-η [-εα]	-εις	-η [-εα]	-έας	-υς

§ 42 First declension (examples)

	1a (fem.)	1b (fem.)	1c (fem.)	1d (masc.)	1e (masc.)
	σπονδή -ῆς ἡ	σοφία -ας ἡ	τόλμα -ης ἡ	ὑβριστής -ου ὁ	νεανίας -ου ὁ
nom. sing.	σπονδή	σοφία	τόλμα	ὑβριστής	νεανίας
gen. sing.	σπονδῆς	σοφίας	τόλμης	ὑβριστοῦ	νεανίου
dat. sing.	σπονδῇ	σοφίᾳ	τόλμῃ	ὑβριστῇ	νεανίᾳ
acc. sing.	σπονδήν	σοφίαν	τόλμαν	ὑβριστήν	νεανίαν
nom. pl.	σπονδαί	σοφίαι	τόλμαι	ὑβρισταί	νεανίαι
gen. pl.	σπονδῶν	σοφιῶν	τολμῶν	ὑβριστῶν	νεανιῶν
dat. pl.	σπονδαῖς	σοφίαις	τόλμαις	ὑβρισταῖς	νεανίαις
acc. pl.	σπονδάς	σοφίας	τόλμας	ὑβριστάς	νεανίας

§ 43 Second declension (examples)

	2a (masc.)	2a (fem.)	2b (neut.)
	θεός -οῦ ὁ	νόσος -ου ἡ	δεῖπνον -ου τό
nom. sing.	θεός	νόσος	δεῖπνον
gen. sing.	θεοῦ	νόσου	δείπνου
dat. sing.	θεῷ	νόσῳ	δείπνῳ
acc. sing.	θεόν	νόσον	δεῖπνον
nom. pl.	θεοί	νόσοι	δεῖπνα
gen. pl.	θεῶν	νόσων	δείπνων
dat. pl.	θεοῖς	νόσοις	δείπνοις
acc. pl.	θεούς	νόσους	δεῖπνα

§ 44 Third declension: consonant stem (examples)

	3a (masc.)	3a (fem.)	3a (masc.)	3b (neut.)
	μάρτυς μάρτυρος ὁ	νύξ νυκτός ἡ	ἀνήρ ἀνδρός ὁ	ὕδωρ ὕδατος τό
nom. sing.	μάρτυς	νύξ	ἀνήρ	ὕδωρ
gen. sing.	μάρτυρος	νυκτός	ἀνδρός	ὕδατος
dat. sing.	μάρτυρι	νυκτί	ἀνδρί	ὕδατι
acc. sing.	μάρτυρα	νύκτα	ἄνδρα	ὕδωρ
nom. pl.	μάρτυρες	νύκτες	ἄνδρες	ὕδατα
gen. pl.	μαρτύρων	νυκτῶν	ἀνδρῶν	ὑδάτων
dat. pl.	μάρτυσι(ν)*	νυξί(ν)	ἀνδράσι(ν)	ὕδασι(ν)
acc. pl.	μάρτυρας	νύκτας	ἄνδρας	ὕδατα

*The absence of rho here is exceptional.

§ 45 Third declension: sigma stem (examples)

- An original sigma in the stem has fallen out between two vowels, with a resulting contraction of two vowels.

	3c (fem.)	3c (masc.)	3d (neut.)	3d (neut.)
	τριήρης -ους ἡ	Περικλῆς -έους ὁ	ἔτος -ους τό	γῆρας -ως τό
nom. sing.	τριήρης	Περικλῆς [-έης]	ἔτος	γῆρας
gen. sing.	τριήρους [-εος]	Περικλέους	ἔτους [-εος]	γήρως [-αος]
dat. sing.	τριήρει	Περικλεῖ	ἔτει	γήραι
acc. sing.	τριήρη [-εα]	Περικλέα	ἔτος	γῆρας
nom. pl.	τριήρεις [-εες]	—	ἔτη [-εα]	γήρα [-αα]
gen. pl.	τριήρων [-εων]	—	ἐτῶν [-έων]	γηρῶν [-άων]
dat. pl.	τριήρεσι(ν)	—	ἔτεσι(ν)	γήρασι(ν)
acc. pl.	τριήρεις	—	ἔτη [-εα]	γήρα [-αα]

§ 46 Third declension: other stems (examples)

	3e (fem.)	3e (masc.)	3f (neut.)	3g (masc.)	3h (masc.)
	πόλις	πρέσβυς	ἄστυ	βασιλεύς	ἰχθύς
	-εως ἡ	-εως ὁ	-εως τό	-έως ὁ	-ύος ὁ
nom. sing.	πόλις	πρέσβυς	ἄστυ	βασιλεύς	ἰχθύς
gen. sing.	πόλεως	πρέσβεως	ἄστεως	βασιλέως	ἰχθύος
dat. sing.	πόλει	πρέσβει	ἄστει	βασιλεῖ	ἰχθύι
acc. sing.	πόλιν	πρέσβυν	ἄστυ	βασιλέα	ἰχθύν
nom. pl.	πόλεις	πρέσβεις	ἄστη	βασιλεῖς/-ῆς	ἰχθύες
gen. pl.	πόλεων	πρέσβεων	ἄστεων	βασιλέων	ἰχθύων
dat. pl.	πόλεσι(ν)	πρέσβεσι(ν)	ἄστεσι(ν)	βασιλεῦσι(ν)	ἰχθύσι(ν)
acc. pl.	πόλεις	πρέσβεις	ἄστη	βασιλέας	ἰχθῦς

§ 47 Third declension: irregular nouns

	ναῦς νέως ἡ	Ζεύς Διός ὁ
nom. sing.	ναῦς	Ζεύς
gen. sing.	νέως	Διός
dat. sing.	νηί	Διί
acc. sing.	ναῦν	Δία
nom. pl.	νῆες	—
gen. pl.	νεῶν	—
dat. pl.	ναυσί(ν)	—
acc. pl.	ναῦς	—

Verbs

§ 48 Summary of verb endings (regular verbs): present/imperfect system

Present active

- present stem (first principal part minus ending) + endings in chart below

	indic.	impera.	subju.	opt.	nonfinite
1st sing.	-ω	—	-ω	-οιμι/-οίην	part. nom. sing. (§26)
2nd sing.	-εις	-ε	-ῃς	-οις/-οίης	*masc.* -ων (-οντ-)
3rd sing.	-ει	-έτω	-ῃ	-οι/-οίη	*fem.* -ουσα
1st pl.	-ομεν	—	-ωμεν	-οιμεν/-οίημεν	*neut.* -ον (-οντ-)
2nd pl.	-ετε	-ετε	-ητε	-οιτε/-οίητε	inf.
3rd pl.	-ουσι(ν)	-όντων	-ωσι(ν)	-οιεν/-οίησαν	-ειν

Present middle-passive

- present stem (first principal part minus ending) + endings in chart below

	indic.	impera.	subju.	opt.	nonfinite
1st sing.	-ομαι	—	-ωμαι	-οίμην	part. nom. sing. (§34)
2nd sing.	-ῃ/-ει	-ου	-ῃ	-οιο	*masc.* -όμενος
3rd sing.	-εται	-έσθω	-ηται	-οιτο	*fem.* -ομένη
1st pl.	-όμεθα	—	-ώμεθα	-οίμεθα	*neut.* -όμενον
2nd pl.	-εσθε	-εσθε	-ησθε	-οισθε	inf.
3rd pl.	-ονται	-έσθων	-ωνται	-οιντο	-εσθαι

Imperfect

- temporal augment + present stem (first principal part minus ending) + endings in chart below

	act. indic.	mid.-pass. indic.
1st sing.	-ον	-όμην
2nd sing.	-ες	-ου
3rd sing.	-ε(ν)	-ετο
1st pl.	-ομεν	-όμεθα
2nd pl.	-ετε	-εσθε
3rd pl.	-ον	-οντο

§ 49 Summary of verb endings: future system

Future active

- future stem (second principal part minus ending) + endings in chart below

	indic.	opt.	nonfinite
1st sing.	-ω	-οιμι	**part. nom. sing. (§29)**
2nd sing.	-εις	-οις	*masc.* -ων (-οντ-)
3rd sing.	-ει	-οι	*fem.* -ουσα
1st pl.	-ομεν	-οιμεν	*neut.* -ον (-οντ-)
2nd pl.	-ετε	-οιτε	**inf.**
3rd pl.	-ουσι(ν)	-οιεν	-ειν

Future middle

- future stem (second principal part minus ending) + endings in chart below

	indic.	opt.	nonfinite
1st sing.	-ομαι	-οίμην	**part. nom. sing. (§36)**
2nd sing.	-η/-ει	-οιο	*masc.* -όμενος
3rd sing.	-εται	-οιτο	*fem.* -ομένη
1st pl.	-όμεθα	-οίμεθα	*neut.* -όμενον
2nd pl.	-εσθε	-οισθε	**inf.**
3rd pl.	-ονται	-οιντο	-εσθαι

Future passive

- aorist passive stem (sixth principal part minus temporal augment and ending) + endings in chart below

	indic.	opt.	nonfinite
1st sing.	-ήσομαι	-ησοίμην	**part. nom. sing. (§36)**
2nd sing.	-ήσῃ/-ήσει	-ήσοιο	*masc.* -ησόμενος
3rd sing.	-ήσεται	-ήσοιτο	*fem.* -ησομένη
1st pl.	-ησόμεθα	-ησοίμεθα	*neut.* -ησόμενον
2nd pl.	-ήσεσθε	-ήσοισθε	**inf.**
3rd pl.	-ήσονται	-ήσοιντο	-ήσεσθαι

§ 50 Summary of verb endings: aorist system

First (weak) aorist active

- for verbs with third principal part ending in -α
  - ≈ aorist stem (third principal part minus temporal augment and ending) + endings in chart below
  - ≈ temporal augment on indicative only

	indic. (aug.)	impera.	subju.	opt.	nonfinite
1st sing.	-α	—	-ω	-αιμι	**part. nom. sing. (§30)**
2nd sing.	-ας	-ον	-ῃς	-αις/-ειας	*masc.* -ας (-αντ-)
3rd sing.	-ε(ν)	-άτω	-ῃ	-αι/-ειε(ν)	*fem.* -ασα
1st pl.	-αμεν	—	-ωμεν	-αιμεν	*neut.* -αν (-αντ-)
2nd pl.	-ατε	-ατε	-ητε	-αιτε	**inf.**
3rd pl.	-αν	-άντων	-ωσι(ν)	-αιεν/-ειαν	-αι

First (weak) aorist middle

- for verbs with third principal part ending in -α or -άμην
  - ≈ aorist stem (third principal part minus temporal augment and ending) + endings in chart below
  - ≈ temporal augment on indicative only

	indic. (aug.)	impera.	subju.	opt.	nonfinite
1st sing.	-άμην	—	-ωμαι	-αίμην	**part. nom. sing. (§37, §34)**
2nd sing.	-ω	-αι	-ῃ	-αιο	*masc.* -άμενος
3rd sing.	-ατο	-άσθω	-ηται	-αιτο	*fem.* -αμένη
1st pl.	-άμεθα	—	-ώμεθα	-αίμεθα	*neut.* -άμενον
2nd pl.	-ασθε	-ασθε	-ησθε	-αισθε	**inf.**
3rd pl.	-αντο	-άσθων	-ωνται	-αιντο	-ασθαι

Aorist passive

- for all verbs
  - ≈ aorist passive stem (sixth principal part minus temporal augment and ending) + endings in chart below
  - ≈ temporal augment on indicative only

	indic. (aug.)	impera.	subju.	opt.	nonfinite
1st sing.	-ην	—	-ῶ	-είην	**part. nom. sing. (§38)**
2nd sing.	-ης	-ητι	-ῇς	-είης	*masc.* -είς (-εντ-)
3rd sing.	-η	-ήτω	-ῇ	-είη	*fem.* -εῖσα
1st pl.	-ημεν	—	-ῶμεν	-εῖμεν	*neut.* -έν (-εντ-)
2nd pl.	-ητε	-ητε	-ῆτε	-εῖτε	**inf.**
3rd pl.	-ησαν	-έντων	-ῶσι(ν)	-εῖεν	-ῆναι

Second (strong) aorist active

- for verbs with third principal part ending in -ov
  - ≈ aorist stem (third principal part minus temporal augment and ending) + endings in chart below
  - ≈ temporal augment on indicative only

	indic. (aug.)	impera.	subju.	opt.	nonfinite
1st sing.	-ον	—	-ω	-οιμι	**part. nom. sing. (§31)**
2nd sing.	-ες	-ε	-ῃς	-οις	*masc.* -ών (-οντ-)
3rd sing.	-ε(ν)	-έτω	-ῃ	-οι	*fem.* -οῦσα
1st pl.	-ομεν	—	-ωμεν	-οιμεν	*neut.* -όν (-οντ-)
2nd pl.	-ετε	-ετε	-ητε	-οιτε	**inf.**
3rd pl.	-ον	-όντων	-ωσι(ν)	-οιεν	-ειν

Second (strong) aorist middle

- for verbs with third principal part ending in -ov or -όμην
  - ≈ aorist stem (third principal part minus temporal augment and ending) + endings in chart below
  - ≈ temporal augment on indicative only

	indic. (aug.)	impera.	subju.	opt.	nonfinite
1st sing.	-όμην	—	-ωμαι	-οίμην	**part. nom. sing. (§34)**
2nd sing.	-ου	-ου	-ῃ	-οιο	*masc.* -όμενος
3rd sing.	-ετο	-έσθω	-ηται	-οιτο	*fem.* -ομένη
1st pl.	-όμεθα	—	-ώμεθα	-οίμεθα	*neut.* -όμενον
2nd pl.	-εσθε	-εσθε	-ησθε	-οισθε	**inf.**
3rd pl.	-οντο	-έσθων	-ωνται	-οιντο	-εσθαι

Root aorist

- for verbs with third principal part ending in -v
  - ≈ aorist stem (third principal part minus temporal augment and ending) + endings in chart below
  - ≈ temporal augment on indicative only

	indic. (aug.)	impera.	subju.	opt.	nonfinite
1st sing.	-ν	—	-ω	-ίην	**part. nom. sing. (§30)**
2nd sing.	-ς	-θι	-ῃς	-ίης	*masc.* -ς (-ντ-)
3rd sing.	—	-τω	-ῃ	-ίη	*fem.* -σα
1st pl.	-μεν	—	-ωμεν	-ῖμεν	*neut.* -ν (-ντ-)
2nd pl.	-τε	-τε	-ητε	-ῖτε	**inf.**
3rd pl.	-σαν	-ντων	-ωσι(ν)	-ῖεν	-ναι

§ 51 Summary of verb endings: perfect system

Perfect active

- perfect active stem (fourth principal part minus ending) + endings in chart below

	indic.	impera.*	subju.*	opt.*	nonfinite
1st sing.	-α	—	-ω	-οιμι	**part. nom. sing. (§33)**
2nd sing.	-ας	-ε	-ῃς	-οις	masc. -ώς (-οτ-)
3rd sing.	-ε(ν)	-έτω	-ῃ	-οι	fem. -υῖα
1st pl.	-αμεν	—	-ωμεν	-οιμεν	neut. -ός (-οτ-)
2nd pl.	-ατε	-ετε	-ητε	-οιτε	**inf.**
3rd pl.	-ασι(ν)	-έτωσαν	-ωσι(ν)	-οιεν	-έναι*

*Or perfect active participle + appropriate form of εἰμί.

Perfect middle-passive

- perfect middle-passive stem (fifth principal part minus ending) + endings in chart below

	indic.	impera.	subju.*	opt.*	nonfinite
1st sing.	-μαι	—	part. + ὦ	part. + εἴην	**part. nom. sing. (§34)**
2nd sing.	-σαι	-σο	part. + ῇς	part. + εἴης	masc. -μενος
3rd sing.	-ται	-σθω	part. + ῇ	part. + εἴη	fem. -μένη
1st pl.	-μεθα	—	part. + ὦμεν	part. + εἶμεν	neut. -μενον
2nd pl.	-σθε	-σθε	part. + ῆτε	part. + εἶτε	**inf.**
3rd pl.	-νται	-σθων	part. + ὦσι	part. + εἶεν	-σθαι

*Perfect middle-passive participle + appropriate form of εἰμί.

Pluperfect active

- temporal augment + perfect active stem (fourth principal part minus ending) + endings in chart below

Pluperfect middle-passive

- temporal augment + perfect middle-passive stem (fifth principal part minus ending) + endings in chart below

	act. indic.	mid.-pass. indic.
1st sing.	-η/-ειν	-μην
2nd sing.	-ης/-εις	-σο
3rd sing.	-ει	-το
1st pl.	-εμεν	-μεθα
2nd pl.	-ετε	-σθε
3rd pl.	-εσαν	-ντο

Future perfect

- occurs only in middle-passive: future perfect middle-passive stem (usually fourth principal part minus -κα) + endings in chart below

	indic.	opt.	nonfinite
1st sing.	-σομαι	-σοίμην	**part. nom. sing. (§34)**
2nd sing.	-ση	-σοιο	*masc.* -σόμενος
3rd sing.	-σεται	-σοιτο	*fem.* -σομένη
1st pl.	-σόμεθα	-σοίμεθα	*neut.* -σόμενον
2nd pl.	-σεσθε	-σοισθε	**inf.**
3rd pl.	-σονται	-σοιντο	-σεσθαι

§ 52 Regular verb (λύω): present/imperfect system

- all forms built on present stem (first principal part minus ending)
- present: present stem + regular endings (§48)
- imperfect: temporal augment + present stem + regular endings (§48)

		act.	mid.-pass.
pres. indic.	1st sing.	λύω	λύομαι
	2nd sing.	λύεις	λύῃ/λύει
	3rd sing.	λύει	λύεται
	1st pl.	λύομεν	λυόμεθα
	2nd pl.	λύετε	λύεσθε
	3rd pl.	λύουσι(ν)	λύονται
pres. impera.	2nd sing.	λῦε	λύου
	3rd sing.	λυέτω	λυέσθω
	2nd pl.	λύετε	λύεσθε
	3rd pl.	λυόντων	λυέσθων
pres. subju.	1st sing.	λύω	λύωμαι
	2nd sing.	λύῃς	λύῃ
	3rd sing.	λύῃ	λύηται
	1st pl.	λύωμεν	λυώμεθα
	2nd pl.	λύητε	λύησθε
	3rd pl.	λύωσι(ν)	λύωνται
pres. opt.	1st sing.	λύοιμι	λυοίμην
	2nd sing.	λύοις	λύοιο
	3rd sing.	λύοι	λύοιτο
	1st pl.	λύοιμεν	λυοίμεθα
	2nd pl.	λύοιτε	λύοισθε
	3rd pl.	λύοιεν	λύοιντο
pres. part.	nom. sing.	λύων -ουσα -ον	λυόμενος -ομένη -όμενον
pres. inf.		λύειν	λύεσθαι
imperf. indic.	1st sing.	ἔλυον	ἐλυόμην
	2nd sing.	ἔλυες	ἐλύου
	3rd sing.	ἔλυε(ν)	ἐλύετο
	1st pl.	ἐλύομεν	ἐλυόμεθα
	2nd pl.	ἐλύετε	ἐλύεσθε
	3rd pl.	ἔλυον	ἐλύοντο

§ 53 Regular verb (λύω): future system

- future active and middle: future stem (second principal part minus ending) + regular endings (§49)
- future passive: aorist passive stem (sixth principal part minus temporal augment and ending) + regular endings (§49)

		act.	mid.	pass.
fut. indic.	1st sing.	λύσω	λύσομαι	λυθήσομαι
	2nd sing.	λύσεις	λύσῃ/λύσει	λυθήσῃ
	3rd sing.	λύσει	λύσεται	λυθήσεται
	1st pl.	λύσομεν	λυσόμεθα	λυθησόμεθα
	2nd pl.	λύσετε	λύσεσθε	λυθήσεσθε
	3rd pl.	λύσουσι(ν)	λύσονται	λυθήσονται
fut. opt.	1st sing.	λύσοιμι	λυσοίμην	λυθησοίμην
	2nd sing.	λύσοις	λύσοιο	λυθήσοιο
	3rd sing.	λύσοι	λύσοιτο	λυθήσοιτο
	1st pl.	λύσοιμεν	λυσοίμεθα	λυθησοίμεθα
	2nd pl.	λύσοιτε	λύσοισθε	λυθήσοισθε
	3rd pl.	λύσοιεν	λύσοιντο	λυθήσοιντο
fut. part.	nom. sing.	λύσων	λυσόμενος	λυθησόμενος
		-ουσα -ον	-η -ον	-η -ον
fut. inf.		λύσειν	λύσεσθαι	λυθήσεσθαι

§ 54 Regular verb (λύω): aorist system (for verbs with first/weak aorist)

- aorist active and middle: aorist stem (third principal part minus temporal augment and ending) + first (weak) aorist endings (§50)
- aorist passive: aorist passive stem (sixth principal part minus temporal augment and ending) + aorist passive endings (§50)
- temporal augment on indicative only

		act.	mid.	pass.
aor. indic.	1st sing.	ἔλυσα	ἐλυσάμην	ἐλύθην
	2nd sing.	ἔλυσας	ἐλύσω	ἐλύθης
	3rd sing.	ἔλυσε(ν)	ἐλύσατο	ἐλύθη
	1st pl.	ἐλύσαμεν	ἐλυσάμεθα	ἐλύθημεν
	2nd pl.	ἐλύσατε	ἐλύσασθε	ἐλύθητε
	3rd pl.	ἔλυσαν	ἐλῦσαντο	ἐλύθησαν
aor. impera.	2nd sing.	λῦσον	λῦσαι	λύθητι
	3rd sing.	λυσάτω	λυσάσθω	λυθήτω
	2nd pl.	λύσατε	λύσασθε	λύθητε
	3rd pl.	λυσάντων	λυσάσθων	λυθέντων
aor. subju.	1st sing.	λύσω	λύσωμαι	λυθῶ
	2nd sing.	λύσῃς	λύσῃ	λυθῇς
	3rd sing.	λύσῃ	λύσηται	λυθῇ
	1st pl.	λύσωμεν	λυσώμεθα	λυθῶμεν
	2nd pl.	λύσητε	λύσησθε	λυθῆτε
	3rd pl.	λύσωσι(ν)	λύσωνται	λυθῶσι(ν)
aor. opt.	1st sing.	λύσαιμι	λυσαίμην	λυθείην
	2nd sing.	λύσαις/λύσειας	λύσαιο	λυθείης
	3rd sing.	λύσαι/λύσειε(ν)	λύσαιτο	λυθείη
	1st pl.	λύσαιμεν	λυσαίμεθα	λυθεῖμεν
	2nd pl.	λύσαιτε	λύσαισθε	λυθεῖτε
	3rd pl.	λύσαιεν/λύσειαν	λύσαιντο	λυθεῖεν
aor. part.	nom. sing.	λύσας	λυσάμενος	λυθείς
		-ασα -αν	-η -ον	-εῖσα -έν
aor. inf.		λῦσαι	λύσασθαι	λυθῆναι

§ 55 Regular verb (λύω): perfect system

- perfect active: perfect active stem (fourth principal part minus ending) + perfect endings (§51)
- perfect middle and passive: perfect middle-passive stem (fifth principal part minus ending) + perfect endings (§51) or (often) perfect middle-passive participle + appropriate form of εἰμί
- temporal augment on pluperfect only
- rare future perfect middle-passive built on reduplicated stem + **-σ-**

		act.	mid.-pass.
perf. indic.	1st sing.	λέλυκα	λέλυμαι
	2nd sing.	λέλυκας	λέλυσαι
	3rd sing.	λέλυκε(ν)	λέλυται
	1st pl.	λελύκαμεν	λελύμεθα
	2nd pl.	λελύκατε	λέλυσθε
	3rd pl.	λελύκασι(ν)	λέλυνται
perf. impera.	2nd sing.	λέλυκε	λέλυσο
	3rd sing.	λελυκέτω	λελύσθω
	2nd pl.	λελύκετε	λέλυσθε
	3rd pl.	λελυκέτωσαν	λελύσθων
perf. subju.	1st sing.	λελύκω	λελυμένος ὦ
	2nd sing.	λελύκῃς	λελυμένος ᾖς
	3rd sing.	λελύκῃ	λελυμένος ᾖ
	1st pl.	λελύκωμεν	λελυμένοι ὦμεν
	2nd pl.	λελύκητε	λελυμένοι ἦτε
	3rd pl.	λελύκωσι(ν)	λελυμένοι ὦσι(ν)
perf. opt.	1st sing.	λελύκοιμι	λελυμένος εἴην
	2nd sing.	λελύκοις	λελυμένος εἴης
	3rd sing.	λελύκοι	λελυμένος εἴη
	1st pl.	λελύκοιμεν	λελυμένοι εἶμεν
	2nd pl.	λελύκοιτε	λελυμένοι εἶτε
	3rd pl.	λελύκοιεν	λελυμένοι εἶεν
perf. part.	nom. sing.	λελυκώς -υῖα -ός	λελυμένος -η -ον
perf. inf.		λελυκέναι	λελῦσθαι

§ 55 Regular verb (λύω): perfect system (continued)

		act.	mid.-pass.
pluperf. indic.	**1st sing.**	ἐλελύκη/ἐλελύκειν*	ἐλελύμην
	2nd sing.	ἐλελύκης/ἐλελύκεις*	ἐλέλυσο
	3rd sing.	ἐλελύκει(ν)/ἐλελύκει*	ἐλέλυτο
	1st pl.	ἐλελύκεμεν	ἐλελύμεθα
	2nd pl.	ἐλελύκετε	ἐλέλυσθε
	3rd pl.	ἐλελύκεσαν	ἐλέλυντο
fut. perf. indic.	**1st sing.**	—	λελύσομαι
	2nd sing.	—	λελύσῃ/λελύσει
	3rd sing.	—	λελύσεται
	1st pl.	—	λελυσόμεθα
	2nd pl.	—	λελύσεσθε
	3rd pl.	—	λελύσονται
fut. perf. opt.	**1st sing.**	—	λελυσοίμην
	2nd sing.	—	λελύσοιο
	3rd sing.	—	λελύσοιτο
	1st pl.	—	λελυσοίμεθα
	2nd pl.	—	λελύσοισθε
	3rd pl.	—	λελύσοιντο
fut. perf. part.	**nom. sing.**	—	λελυσόμενος -η -ον
fut. perf. inf.		—	λελύσεσθαι

*Late variants.

§ 56 Verb with second (strong) aorist (λαμβάνω): aorist system

- for verbs with third principal part ending in -ον or -όμην (e.g., λαμβάνω λήψομαι **ἔλαβον** εἴληφα εἴλημμαι ἐλήφθην)
- aorist active and middle: aorist stem (third principal part minus temporal augment and ending) + second (strong) aorist endings (§50)
- aorist passive: aorist passive stem (sixth principal part minus temporal augment and ending) + regular aorist endings (§50) (i.e., like to aorist passive forms of other types of verb)
- temporal augment on indicative only

		act.	mid.	pass.
aor. indic.	1st sing.	ἔλαβον	ἐλαβόμην	ἐλήφθην
	2nd sing.	ἔλαβες	ἐλάβου	ἐλήφθης
	3rd sing.	ἔλαβε(ν)	ἐλάβετο	ἐλήφθη
	1st pl.	ἐλάβομεν	ἐλαβόμεθα	ἐλήφθημεν
	2nd pl.	ἐλάβετε	ἐλάβεσθε	ἐλήφθητε
	3rd pl.	ἔλαβον	ἐλάβοντο	ἐλήφθησαν
aor. impera.	2nd sing.	λαβέ	λαβοῦ	λήφθητι
	3rd sing.	λαβέτω	λαβέσθω	ληφθήτω
	2nd pl.	λάβετε	λάβεσθε	λήφθητε
	3rd pl.	λαβόντων	λαβέσθων	ληφθέντων
aor. subju.	1st sing.	λάβω	λάβωμαι	ληφθῶ
	2nd sing.	λάβῃς	λάβῃ	ληφθῇς
	3rd sing.	λάβῃ	λάβηται	ληφθῇ
	1st pl.	λάβωμεν	λαβώμεθα	ληφθῶμεν
	2nd pl.	λάβητε	λάβησθε	ληφθῆτε
	3rd pl.	λάβωσι(ν)	λάβωνται	ληφθῶσι(ν)
aor. opt.	1st sing.	λάβοιμι	λαβοίμην	ληφθείην
	2nd sing.	λάβοις	λάβοιο	ληφθείης
	3rd sing.	λάβοι	λάβοιτο	ληφθείη
	1st pl.	λάβοιμεν	λαβοίμεθα	ληφθεῖμεν
	2nd pl.	λάβοιτε	λάβοισθε	ληφθεῖτε
	3rd pl.	λάβοιεν	λάβοιντο	ληφθεῖεν
aor. part.	nom. sing.	λαβών	λαβόμενος	ληφθείς
		-οῦσα -όν	-η -ον	-εῖσα -έν
aor. inf.		λαβεῖν	λαβέσθαι	ληφθῆναι

§ 57 Alpha-contract verb (ἐράω): present/imperfect system

		act.	mid.-pass.
pres. indic.	1st sing.	ἐρῶ [-άω]	ἐρῶμαι [-άομαι]
	2nd sing.	ἐρᾷς [-άεις]	ἐρᾷ [-άει/-άῃ]
	3rd sing.	ἐρᾷ [-άει]	ἐρᾶται [-άεται]
	1st pl.	ἐρῶμεν [-άομεν]	ἐρώμεθα [-αόμεθα]
	2nd pl.	ἐρᾶτε [-άετε]	ἐρᾶσθε [-άεσθε]
	3rd pl.	ἐρῶσι(ν) [-άουσι]	ἐρῶνται [-άονται]
pres. impera.	2nd sing.	ἔρα [-αε]	ἐρῶ [-άου]
	3rd sing.	ἐράτω [-αέτω]	ἐράσθω [-αέσθω]
	2nd pl.	ἐρᾶτε [-άετε]	ἐρᾶσθε [-άεσθε]
	3rd pl.	ἐρώντων [-αόντων]	ἐράσθων [-αέσθων]
pres. subju.	1st sing.	ἐρῶ [-άω]	ἐρῶμαι [-άωμαι]
	2nd sing.	ἐρᾷς [-άῃς]	ἐρᾷ [-άῃ/-άει]
	3rd sing.	ἐρᾷ [-άῃ]	ἐρᾶται [-άηται]
	1st pl.	ἐρῶμεν [-άωμεν]	ἐρώμεθα [-αώμεθα]
	2nd pl.	ἐρᾶτε [-άητε]	ἐρᾶσθε [-άησθε]
	3rd pl.	ἐρῶσι(ν) [-άωσι]	ἐρῶνται [-άωνται]
pres. opt.	1st sing.	ἐρῴην [-αοίην]	ἐρῴμην [-αοίμην]
	2nd sing.	ἐρῴης [-αοίης]	ἐρῷο [-άοιο]
	3rd sing.	ἐρῴη [-αοίη]	ἐρῷτο [-άοιτο]
	1st pl.	ἐρῷμεν [-άοιμεν]	ἐρῴμεθα [-αοίμεθα]
	2nd pl.	ἐρῷτε [-άοιτε]	ἐρῷσθε [-άοισθε]
	3rd pl.	ἐρῷεν [-άοιεν]	ἐρῷντο [-άοιντο]
pres. part.	nom. sing.	ἐρῶν -ῶσα -ῶν	ἐρώμενος -η -ον
		[-άων -άουσα -άον]	[-αόμενος -η -ον]
pres. inf.		ἐρᾶν [-άεεν]*	ἐρᾶσθαι [-άεσθαι]
imperf. indic.	1st sing.	ἤρων [-αον]	ἠρώμην [-αόμην]
	2nd sing.	ἤρας [-αες]	ἠρῶ [-άου]
	3rd sing.	ἤρα [-αε]	ἠρᾶτο [-άετο]
	1st pl.	ἠρῶμεν [-άομεν]	ἠρώμεθα [-αόμεθα]
	2nd pl.	ἠρᾶτε [-άετε]	ἠρᾶσθε [-άεσθε]
	3rd pl.	ἤρων [-αον]	ἠρῶντο [-άοντο]

*The infinitive ending -εɩν was originally -εεν.

§ 58 Epsilon-contract verb (φιλέω): present/imperfect system

		act.	mid.-pass.
pres. indic.	1st sing.	φιλῶ [-έω]	φιλοῦμαι [-έομαι]
	2nd sing.	φιλεῖς [-έεις]	φιλῇ/φιλεῖ [-έῃ/-έει]
	3rd sing.	φιλεῖ [-έει]	φιλεῖται [-έεται]
	1st pl.	φιλοῦμεν [-έομεν]	φιλούμεθα [-εόμεθα]
	2nd pl.	φιλεῖτε [-έετε]	φιλεῖσθε [-έεσθε]
	3rd pl.	φιλοῦσι(ν) [-έουσι]	φιλοῦνται [-έονται]
pres. impera.	2nd sing.	φίλει [-εε]	φιλοῦ [-έου]
	3rd sing.	φιλείτω [-εέτω]	φιλείσθω [-εέσθω]
	2nd pl.	φιλεῖτε [-έετε]	φιλεῖσθε [-έεσθε]
	3rd pl.	φιλούντων [-εόντων]	φιλείσθων [-εέσθων]
pres. subju.	1st sing.	φιλῶ [-έω]	φιλῶμαι [-έωμαι]
	2nd sing.	φιλῇς [-έῃς]	φιλῇ [-έῃ]
	3rd sing.	φιλῇ [-έῃ]	φιλῆται [-έηται]
	1st pl.	φιλῶμεν [-έωμεν]	φιλώμεθα [-εώμεθα]
	2nd pl.	φιλῆτε [-έητε]	φιλῆσθε [-έησθε]
	3rd pl.	φιλῶσι(ν) [-έωσι]	φιλῶνται [-έωνται]
pres. opt.	1st sing.	φιλοίην [-εοίην]	φιλοίμην [-εοίμην]
	2nd sing.	φιλοίης [-εοίης]	φιλοῖο [-έοιο]
	3rd sing.	φιλοίη [-εοίη]	φιλοῖτο [-έοιτο]
	1st pl.	φιλοῖμεν [-έοιμεν]	φιλοίμεθα [-εοίμεθα]
	2nd pl.	φιλοῖτε [-έοιτε]	φιλοῖσθε [-έοισθε]
	3rd pl.	φιλοῖεν [-έοιεν]	φιλοῖντο [-έοιντο]
pres. part.	nom. sing.	φιλῶν -οῦσα -οῦν [-έων -έουσα -έον]	φιλούμενος -η -ον [-εόμενος -η -ον]
pres. inf.		φιλεῖν [-έειν]	φιλεῖσθαι [-έεσθαι]
imperf. indic.	1st sing.	ἐφίλουν [-εον]	ἐφιλούμην [-εόμην]
	2nd sing.	ἐφίλεις [-εες]	ἐφιλοῦ [-έου]
	3rd sing.	ἐφίλει [-εε]	ἐφιλεῖτο [-έετο]
	1st pl.	ἐφιλοῦμεν [-έομεν]	ἐφιλούμεθα [-εόμεθα]
	2nd pl.	ἐφιλεῖτε [-έετε]	ἐφιλεῖσθε [-έεσθε]
	3rd pl.	ἐφίλουν [-εον]	ἐφιλοῦντο [-έοντο]

§ 59 Omicron-contract verb (δηλόω): present/imperfect system

		act.	mid.-pass.
pres. indic.	1st sing.	δηλῶ [-όω]	δηλοῦμαι [-όομαι]
	2nd sing.	δηλοῖς [-όεις]	δηλοῖ [-όει/-όῃ]
	3rd sing.	δηλοῖ [-όει]	δηλοῦται [-όεται]
	1st pl.	δηλοῦμεν [-όομεν]	δηλούμεθα [-οόμεθα]
	2nd pl.	δηλοῦτε [-όετε]	δηλοῦσθε [-όεσθε]
	3rd pl.	δηλοῦσι(ν) [-όουσι]	δηλοῦνται [-όονται]
pres. impera.	2nd sing.	δήλου [-οε]	δηλοῦ [-όου]
	3rd sing.	δηλούτω [-οέτω]	δηλούσθω [-οέσθω]
	2nd pl.	δηλοῦτε [-όετε]	δηλοῦσθε [-όεσθε]
	3rd pl.	δηλούντων [-οόντων]	δηλούσθων [-οέσθων]
pres. subju.	1st sing.	δηλῶ [-όω]	δηλῶμαι [-όωμαι]
	2nd sing.	δηλοῖς [-όῃς]	δηλοῖ [-όῃ]
	3rd sing.	δηλοῖ [-όῃ]	δηλῶται [-όηται]
	1st pl.	δηλῶμεν [-όωμεν]	δηλώμεθα [-οώμεθα]
	2nd pl.	δηλῶτε [-όητε]	δηλῶσθε [-όησθε]
	3rd pl.	δηλῶσι(ν) [-όωσι]	δηλῶνται [-όωνται]
pres. opt.	1st sing.	δηλοίην [-οοίην]	δηλοίμην [-οοίμην]
	2nd sing.	δηλοίης [-οοίης]	δηλοῖο [-όοιο]
	3rd sing.	δηλοίη [-οοίη]	δηλοῖτο [-όοιτο]
	1st pl.	δηλοῖμεν [-όοιμεν]	δηλοίμεθα [-οοίμεθα]
	2nd pl.	δηλοῖτε [-όοιτε]	δηλοῖσθε [-όοισθε]
	3rd pl.	δηλοῖεν [-όοιεν]	δηλοῖντο [-όοιντο]
pres. part.	nom. sing.	δηλῶν -οῦσα -οῦν	δηλούμενος -η -ον
		[-όων -όουσα -όον]	[-οόμενος -η -ον]
pres. inf.		δηλοῦν [-όεεν]*	δηλοῦσθαι [-όεσθαι]
imperf. indic.	1st sing.	ἐδήλουν [-οον]	ἐδηλούμην [-οόμην]
	2nd sing.	ἐδήλους [-οες]	ἐδηλοῦ [-όου]
	3rd sing.	ἐδήλου [-οε]	ἐδηλοῦτο [-όετο]
	1st pl.	ἐδηλοῦμεν [-όομεν]	ἐδηλούμεθα [-οόμεθα]
	2nd pl.	ἐδηλοῦτε [-όετε]	ἐδηλοῦσθε [-όεσθε]
	3rd pl.	ἐδήλουν [-οον]	ἐδηλοῦντο [-όοντο]

*The infinitive ending -ειν was originally -εεν.

§ 60 Athematic (-μι) verbs: present/imperfect system

		δίδωμι (give)	τίθημι (put)	δείκνυμι (show)	ἵστημι (set)	ἵημι (send)
pres. act. indic.	1st sing.	δίδωμι	τίθημι	δείκνυμι	ἵστημι	ἵημι
	2nd sing.	δίδως	τίθης	δείκνυς	ἵστης	ἵης
	3rd sing.	δίδωσι(ν)	τίθησι(ν)	δείκνυσι(ν)	ἵστησι(ν)	ἵησι(ν)
	1st pl.	δίδομεν	τίθεμεν	δείκνυμεν	ἵσταμεν	ἵεμεν
	2nd pl.	δίδοτε	τίθετε	δείκνυτε	ἵστατε	ἵετε
	3rd pl.	διδόασι(ν)	τιθέασι(ν)	δεικνύασι(ν)	ἱστᾶσι(ν)	ἱᾶσι(ν)
pres. act. impera.	2nd sing.	δίδου [-οε]	τίθει [-εε]	δείκνυ [-υε]	ἵστη [-ηε]	ἵει [-εε]
	3rd sing.	διδότω	τιθέτω	δεικνύτω	ἱστάτω	ἱέτω
	2nd pl.	δίδοτε	τίθετε	δείκνυτε	ἵστατε	ἵετε
	3rd pl.	διδόντων	τιθέντων	δεικνύντων	ἱστάντων	ἱέντων
pres. act. subju.	1st sing.	διδῶ	τιθῶ	δεικνύω	ἱστῶ	ἱῶ
	2nd sing.	διδῷς	τιθῇς	δεικνύῃς	ἱστῇς	ἱῇς
	3rd sing.	διδῷ	τιθῇ	δεικνύῃ	ἱστῇ	ἱῇ
	1st pl.	διδῶμεν	τιθῶμεν	δεικνύωμεν	ἱστῶμεν	ἱῶμεν
	2nd pl.	διδῶτε	τιθῆτε	δεικνύητε	ἱστῆτε	ἱῆτε
	3rd pl.	διδῶσι(ν)	τιθῶσι(ν)	δεικνύωσι(ν)	ἱστῶσι(ν)	ἱῶσι(ν)
pres. act. opt.	1st sing.	διδοίην	τιθείην	δεικνύοιμι	ἱσταίην	ἱείην
	2nd sing.	διδοίης	τιθείης	δεικνύοις	ἱσταίης	ἱείης
	3rd sing.	διδοίη	τιθείη	δεικνύοι	ἱσταίη	ἱείη
	1st pl.	διδοῖμεν	τιθεῖμεν	δεικνύοιμεν	ἱσταῖμεν	ἱεῖμεν
	2nd pl.	διδοῖτε	τιθεῖτε	δεικνύοιτε	ἱσταῖτε	ἱεῖτε
	3rd pl.	διδοῖεν	τιθεῖεν	δεικνύοιεν	ἱσταῖεν	ἱεῖεν
pres. act. part. nom. sing. (§28, §26)	masc.	διδούς (διδόντ-)	τιθείς (τιθέντ-)	δεικνύς (δεικνύντ-)	ἱστάς (ἱστάντ-)	ἱείς (ἱέντ-)
	fem.	διδοῦσα	τιθεῖσα	δεικνῦσα	ἱστᾶσα	ἱεῖσα
	neut.	διδόν	τιθέν	δεικνύν	ἱστάν	ἱέν
pres. act. inf.		διδόναι	τιθέναι	δεικνύναι	ἱστάναι	ἱέναι

i§ 60 Athematic (-μι) verbs: present/imperfect system (continued)

		δίδωμι (give)	τίθημι (put)	δείκνυμι (show)	ἵστημι (set)	ἵημι (send)
imperf. act. indic.	1st sing.	ἐδίδουν	ἐτίθην	ἐδείκνυν	ἵστην	ἵην
	2nd sing.	ἐδίδους	ἐτίθεις	ἐδείκνυς	ἵστης	ἵεις
	3rd sing.	ἐδίδου	ἐτίθει	ἐδείκνυ	ἵστη	ἵει
	1st pl.	ἐδίδομεν	ἐτίθεμεν	ἐδείκνυμεν	ἵσταμεν	ἵεμεν
	2nd pl.	ἐδίδοτε	ἐτίθετε	ἐδείκνυτε	ἵστατε	ἵετε
	3rd pl.	ἐδίδοσαν	ἐτίθεσαν	ἐδείκνυσαν	ἵστασαν	ἵεσαν
pres. mid.-pass. indic.	1st sing.	δίδομαι	τίθεμαι	δείκνυμαι	ἵσταμαι	ἵεμαι
	2nd sing.	δίδοσαι	τίθεσαι	δείκνυσαι	ἵστασαι	ἵεσαι
	3rd sing.	δίδοται	τίθεται	δείκνυται	ἵσταται	ἵεται
	1st pl.	διδόμεθα	τιθέμεθα	δεικνύμεθα	ἱστάμεθα	ἱέμεθα
	2nd pl.	δίδοσθε	τίθεσθε	δείκνυσθε	ἵστασθε	ἵεσθε
	3rd pl.	δίδονται	τίθενται	δείκνυνται	ἵστανται	ἵενται
pres. mid.-pass. impera.	2nd sing.	δίδοσο	τίθεσο	δείκνυσο	ἵστασο	ἵεσο
	3rd sing.	διδόσθω	τιθέσθω	δεικνύσθω	ἱστάσθω	ἱέσθω
	2nd pl.	δίδοσθε	τίθεσθε	δείκνυσθε	ἵστασθε	ἵεσθε
	3rd pl.	διδόσθων	τιθέσθων	δεικνύσθων	ἱστάσθων	ἱέσθων
pres. mid.-pass. subju.	1st sing.	διδῶμαι	τιθῶμαι	δεικνύωμαι	ἱστῶμαι	ἱῶμαι
	2nd sing.	διδῷ	τιθῇ	δεικνύῃ	ἱστῇ	ἱῇ
	3rd sing.	διδῶται	τιθῆται	δεικνύηται	ἱστῆται	ἱῆται
	1st pl.	διδώμεθα	τιθώμεθα	δεικνυώμεθα	ἱστώμεθα	ἱώμεθα
	2nd pl.	διδῶσθε	τιθῆσθε	δεικνύησθε	ἱστῆσθε	ἱῆσθε
	3rd pl.	διδῶνται	τιθῶνται	δεικνύωνται	ἱστῶνται	ἱῶνται

§ 60 Athematic (-μι) verbs: present/imperfect system (continued)

		δίδωμι (give)	τίθημι (put)	δείκνυμι (show)	ἵστημι (set)	ἵημι (send)
pres. mid.-pass. opt.	1st sing.	διδοίμην	τιθείμην	δεικνυοίμην	ἱσταίμην	ἱείμην
	2nd sing.	διδοῖο	τιθεῖο	δεικνύοιο	ἱσταῖο	ἱεῖο
	3rd sing.	διδοῖτο	τιθεῖτο	δεικνύοιτο	ἱσταῖτο	ἱεῖτο
	1st pl.	διδοίμεθα	τιθείμεθα	δεικνυοίμεθα	ἱσταίμεθα	ἱείμεθα
	2nd pl.	διδοῖσθε	τιθεῖσθε	δεικνύοισθε	ἱσταῖσθε	ἱεῖσθε
	3rd pl.	διδοῖντο	τιθεῖντο	δεικνύοιντο	ἱσταῖντο	ἱεῖντο
pres. mid.-pass. part. (§35, §34)	nom. sing.	διδόμενος -η -ον	τιθέμενος -η -ον	δεικνύμενος -η -ον	ἱστάμενος -η -ον	ἱέμενος -η -ον
pres. mid.-pass. inf.		δίδοσθαι	τίθεσθαι	δείκνυσθαι	ἵστασθαι	ἵεσθαι
imperf. mid.-pass. indic.	1st sing.	ἐδιδόμην	ἐτιθέμην	ἐδεικνύμην	ἱστάμην	ἱέμην
	2nd sing.	ἐδίδοσο	ἐτίθεσο	ἐδείκνυσο	ἵστασο	ἵεσο
	3rd sing.	ἐδίδοτο	ἐτίθετο	ἐδείκνυτο	ἵστατο	ἵετο
	1st pl.	ἐδιδόμεθα	ἐτιθέμεθα	ἐδεικνύμεθα	ἱστάμεθα	ἱέμεθα
	2nd pl.	ἐδίδοσθε	ἐτίθεσθε	ἐδείκνυσθε	ἵστασθε	ἵεσθε
	3rd pl.	ἐδίδοντο	ἐτίθεντο	ἐδείκνυντο	ἵσταντο	ἵεντο

§ 61 Athematic (-μι) verbs: future system

- use regular endings (§49, §53)
- learn principal parts

	δίδομι (give)	τίθημι (put)	δείκνυμι (show)	ἵστημι (set)	ἵημι (send)
fut. act.	δώσω	θήσω	δείξω	στήσω	*-ἥσω
fut. mid.	δώσομαι	θήσομαι	δείξομαι	στήσομαι	*-ἥσομαι
fut. pass.	δοθήσομαι	τεθήσομαι	δειχθήσομαι	σταθήσομαι	*-ἐθήσομαι

§62 Athematic (-μι) verbs: aorist system

- Δείκνυμι and ἵστημι (transitive) use regular first (weak) aorist endings (§50, §54) (learn stems).

		δίδωμι (give)	τίθημι (put)	δείκνυμι (show)	ἵστημι (set)	ἵημι (send)
aor. act. indic.	**1st sing.**	ἔδωκα	ἔθηκα	ἔδειξα	ἔστησα	*-ἧκα
	2nd sing.	ἔδωκας	ἔθηκας	ἔδειξας	ἔστησας	*-ἧκας
	3rd sing.	ἔδωκε(ν)	ἔθηκε(ν)	ἔδειξε(ν)	ἔστησε(ν)	*-ἧκε(ν)
	1st pl.	ἔδομεν	ἔθεμεν	ἐδείξαμεν	ἐστήσαμεν	*-εἷμεν
	2nd pl.	ἔδοτε	ἔθετε	ἐδείξατε	ἐστήσατε	*-εἷτε
	3rd pl.	ἔδοσαν	ἔθεσαν	ἔδειξαν	ἔστησαν	*-εἷσαν
aor. act. impera.	**2nd sing.**	δός	θές	δεῖξον	στῆσον	*-ἕς
	3rd sing.	δότω	θέτω	δειξάτω	στησάτω	*-ἕτω
	2nd pl.	δότε	θέτε	δείξατε	στήσατε	*-ἕτε
	3rd pl.	δόντων	θέντων	δειξάντων	στησάντων	*-ἕντων
aor. act. subju.	**1st sing.**	δῶ	θῶ	δείξω	στήσω	*-ὧ
	2nd sing.	δῷς	θῇς	δείξῃς	στήσῃς	*-ἧς
	3rd sing.	δῷ	θῇ	δείξῃ	στήσῃ	*-ἧ
	1st pl.	δῶμεν	θῶμεν	δείξωμεν	στήσωμεν	*-ὧμεν
	2nd pl.	δῶτε	θῆτε	δείξητε	στήσητε	*-ἧτε
	3rd pl.	δῶσι(ν)	θῶσι(ν)	δείξωσι(ν)	στήσωσι(ν)	*-ὧσι(ν)
aor. act. opt.	**1st sing.**	δοίην	θείην	δείξαιμι	στήσαιμι	*-εἵην
	2nd sing.	δοίης	θείης	δείξαις/δείξειας	στήσαις/στήσειας	*-εἵης
	3rd sing.	δοίη	θείη	δείξαι/δείξειε(ν)	στήσαι/στήσειε(ν)	*-εἵη
	1st pl.	δοῖμεν	θεῖμεν	δείξαιμεν	στήσαιμεν	*-εἷμεν
	2nd pl.	δοῖτε	θεῖτε	δείξαιτε	στήσαιτε	*-εἷτε
	3rd pl.	δοῖεν	θεῖεν	δείξαιεν/δείξειαν	στήσαιεν/στήσειαν	*-εἷεν
aor. act. part. nom. sing. (§§30–32)	**masc.**	δούς (δοντ-)	θείς (θεντ-)	δείξας (δειξαντ-)	στήσαιεν/στήσειαν	*-εἵς (*-ἑντ-)
	fem.	δοῦσα	θεῖσα	δείξασα	στήσασα	*-εἷσα
	neut.	δόν (δοντ-)	θέν (θεντ-)	δεῖξαν (δειξαντ-)	στῆσαν (στησαντ-)	*-ἕν (*-ἑντ-)

41

§ 62 Athematic (-μι) verbs: aorist system (continued)

		δίδωμι (give)	τίθημι (put)	δείκνυμι (show)	ἵστημι (set)	ἵημι (send)
aor. act. inf.		δοῦναι	θεῖναι	δεῖξαι	στῆσαι	*-εἷναι
aor. mid. indic.	**1st sing.**	ἐδόμην	ἐθέμην	ἐδειξάμην	ἐστησάμην	*-εἵμην
	2nd sing.	ἔδου	ἔθου	ἐδείξω	ἐστήσω	*-εἷσο
	3rd sing.	ἔδοτο	ἔθετο	ἐδείξατο	ἐστήσατο	*-εἷτο
	1st pl.	ἐδόμεθα	ἐθέμεθα	ἐδειξάμεθα	ἐστησάμεθα	*-εἵμεθα
	2nd pl.	ἔδοσθε	ἔθεσθε	ἐδείξασθε	ἐστήσασθε	*-εἷσθε
	3rd pl.	ἔδοντο	ἔθεντο	ἐδείξαντο	ἐστήσαντο	*-εἷντο
aor. mid. impera.	**2nd sing.**	δοῦ	θοῦ	δεῖξαι	στῆσαι	*-οὗ
	3rd sing.	δόσθω	θέσθω	δειξάσθω	στησάσθω	*-ἕσθω
	2nd pl.	δόσθε	θέσθε	δείξασθε	στήσασθε	*-ἕσθε
	3rd pl.	δόσθων	θέσθων	δειξάσθων	στησάσθων	*-ἕσθων
aor. mid. subju.	**1st sing.**	δῶμαι	θῶμαι	δείξωμαι	στήσωμαι	*-ὧμαι
	2nd sing.	δῷ	θῇ	δείξῃ	στήσῃ	*-ᾗ
	3rd sing.	δῶται	θῆται	δείξηται	στήσηται	*-ἧται
	1st pl.	δώμεθα	θώμεθα	δειξώμεθα	στησώμεθα	*-ὥμεθα
	2nd pl.	δῶσθε	θῆσθε	δείξησθε	στήσησθε	*-ἧσθε
	3rd pl.	δῶνται	θῶνται	δείξωνται	στήσωνται	*-ὧνται
aor. mid. opt.	**1st sing.**	δοίμην	θείμην	δειξαίμην	στησαίμην	*-εἵμην
	2nd sing.	δοῖο	θεῖο	δείξαιο	στήσαιο	*-εἷο
	3rd sing.	δοῖτο	θεῖτο	δείξαιτο	στήσαιτο	*-εἷτο
	1st pl.	δοίμεθα	θείμεθα	δειξαίμεθα	στησαίμεθα	*-εἵμεθα
	2nd pl.	δοῖσθε	θεῖσθε	δείξαισθε	στήσαισθε	*-εἷσθε
	3rd pl.	δοῖντο	θεῖντο	δείξαιντο	στήσαιντο	*-εἷντο
aor. mid. part. nom. sing. (§37, §34)		δόμενος, -η -ον	θέμενος, -η -ον	δειξάμενος, -η -ον	στησάμενος, -η -ον	*-ἕμενος, -η -ον
aor. mid. inf.		δόσθαι	θέσθαι	δείξασθαι	στήσασθαι	*-ἕσθαι
aor. pass.† indic.	**1st sing.**	ἐδόθην etc.	ἐτέθην etc.	ἐδείχθην etc.	ἐστάθην etc.	*-εἵθην† (-ἑθ-) etc.

†Aorist passive is perfectly regular (§50, §54). Learn sixth principal parts.

42

§ 63 Athematic (-μι) verbs: perfect system

- learn principal parts
- regular (§51, §55) except for active forms of ἵστημι

	δίδωμι (give)	τίθημι (put)	δείκνυμι (show)	ἵστημι (set)	ἵημι (send)
perf. act.	δέδωκα	τέθηκα	δέδειχα	ἕστηκα	*-εἷκα
perf. mid.-pass.	δέδομαι	τέθημαι	δέδειγμαι	ἕσταμαι	*-εἷμαι

- perfect active: ἵστημι

	indic.	subju.	impera.	opt.	nonfinite
1st sing.	ἕστηκα	ἑστῶ	—	ἑσταίην	**part. nom. sing.**
2nd sing.	ἕστηκας	ἑστῇς	ἕσταθι	ἑσταίης	*masc.* ἑστώς
3rd sing.	ἕστηκε(ν)	ἑστῇ	ἑστάτω	ἑσταίη	*fem.* ἑστῶσα
1st pl.	ἕσταμεν	ἑστῶμεν	—	ἑσταίμεν	*neut.* ἑστός
2nd pl.	ἕστατε	ἑστῆτε	ἕστατε	ἑσταῖτε	**inf.**
3rd pl.	ἑστᾶσι(ν)	ἑστῶσι	ἑστάντων	ἑσταῖεν	ἑστάναι

§ 64 Verbs with root aorist (e.g., ἔγνων from γιγνώσκω, ἔβην from βαίνω, ἔστην from ἵστημι): aorist system

- active forms only
- identifiable from third principal part
- temporal augment on indicative only

		γιγνώσκω	βαίνω	ἵστημι
aor. indic.	1st sing.	ἔγνων	ἔβην	ἔστην
	2nd sing.	ἔγνως	ἔβης	ἔστης
	3rd sing.	ἔγνω	ἔβη	ἔστη
	1st pl.	ἔγνωμεν	ἔβημεν	ἔστημεν
	2nd pl.	ἔγνωτε	ἔβητε	ἔστητε
	3rd pl.	ἔγνωσαν	ἔβησαν	ἔστησαν
aor. impera.	2nd sing.	γνῶθι	βῆθι	στῆθι
	3rd sing.	γνώτω	βήτω	στήτω
	2nd pl.	γνῶτε	βῆτε	στῆτε
	3rd pl.	γνόντων	βάντων	στάντων
aor. subju.	1st sing.	γνῶ	βῶ	στῶ
	2nd sing.	γνῷς	βῇς	στῇς
	3rd sing.	γνῷ	βῇ	στῇ
	1st pl.	γνῶμεν	βῶμεν	στῶμεν
	2nd pl.	γνῶτε	βῆτε	στῆτε
	3rd pl.	γνῶσι(ν)	βῶσι(ν)	στῶσι(ν)
aor. opt.	1st sing.	γνοίην	βαίην	σταίην
	2nd sing.	γνοίης	βαίης	σταίης
	3rd sing.	γνοίη	βαίη	σταίη
	1st pl.	γνοῖμεν	βαῖμεν	σταῖμεν
	2nd pl.	γνοῖτε	βαῖτε	σταῖτε
	3rd pl.	γνοῖεν	βαῖεν	σταῖεν
aor. part. nom.	masc.	γνούς (γνοντ-)	βάς (βαντ-)	στάς (σταντ-)
sing. (§32, §31)	fem.	γνοῦσα	βᾶσα	στᾶσα
	neut.	γνόν (γνοντ-)	βάν (βαντ-)	στάν (σταντ-)
aor. inf.		γνῶναι	βῆναι	στῆναι

§ 65 Irregular verbs: present/imperfect system

		εἰμί (be)	οἶδα (know)	εἶμι (go)	φημί (say)
pres. indic.	1st sing.	εἰμί	οἶδα	—	φημί
	2nd sing.	εἶ	οἶσθα	—	φής, φής
	3rd sing.	ἐστί(ν)	οἶδε(ν)	—	φησί(ν)
	1st pl.	ἐσμέν	ἴσμεν	—	φαμέν
	2nd pl.	ἐστέ	ἴστε	—	φατέ
	3rd pl.	εἰσί(ν)	ἴσασι(ν)	—	φασί(ν)
pres. impera.	2nd sing.	ἴσθι	ἴσθι	ἴθι	φάθι
	3rd sing.	ἔστω	ἴστω	ἴτω	φάτω
	2nd pl.	ἔστε	ἴστε	ἴτε	φάτε
	3rd pl.	ἔστων/ ὄντων	ἴστων	ἰόντων	φάντων
pres. subju.	1st sing.	ὦ	εἰδῶ	ἴω	φῶ
	2nd sing.	ἦς	εἰδῆς	ἴῃς	φῆς
	3rd sing.	ἦ	εἰδῇ	ἴῃ	φῇ
	1st pl.	ὦμεν	εἰδῶμεν	ἴωμεν	φῶμεν
	2nd pl.	ἦτε	εἰδῆτε	ἴητε	φῆτε
	3rd pl.	ὦσι(ν)	εἰδῶσι(ν)	ἴωσι(ν)	φῶσι(ν)
pres. opt.	1st sing.	εἴην	εἰδείην	ἴοιμι	φαίην
	2nd sing.	εἴης	εἰδείης	ἴοις	φαίης
	3rd sing.	εἴη	εἰδείη	ἴοι	φαίη
	1st pl.	εἶμεν	εἰδεῖμεν	ἴοιμεν	φαῖμεν
	2nd pl.	εἶτε	εἰδεῖτε	ἴοιτε	φαῖτε
	3rd pl.	εἶεν	εἰδεῖεν	ἴοιεν	φαῖεν
pres. part. nom. sing. (§25, §33, §26)	masc.	ὤν (ὀντ-)	εἰδώς (εἰδοτ-)	ἰών (ἰοντ-)	φάσκων (φασκοντ-)
	fem.	οὖσα	εἰδυῖα	ἰοῦσα	φάσκουσα
	neut.	ὄν (ὀντ-)	εἰδός (εἰδοτ-)	ἰόν (ἰοντ-)	φάσκον (φασκοντ-)
pres. inf.		εἶναι	εἰδέναι	ἰέναι	φάναι
imperf. indic.	1st sing.	ἦ/ἦν	ᾔδη	ᾖα/ᾔειν	ἔφην
	2nd sing.	ἦσθα	ᾔδησθα	ᾔεισθα/ ᾔεις	ἔφησθα/ ἔφης
	3rd sing.	ἦν	ᾔδει (ν)	ᾔει (ν)	ἔφη
	1st pl.	ἦμεν	ᾖσμεν	ᾖμεν	ἔφαμεν
	2nd pl.	ἦτε/ἦστε	ᾖστε	ᾖτε	ἔφατε
	3rd pl.	ἦσαν	ᾖσαν/ ᾔδεσαν	ᾖσαν/ ᾔεσαν	ἔφασαν

§ 66 Irregular verbs: future system

• With the exception of boldface forms, these use regular endings.

		εἰμί (be)	οἶδα (know)	εἶμι (go)	φημί (say)
fut. indic.	**1st sing.**	ἔσομαι	εἴσομαι	**εἶμι**	φήσω
	2nd sing.	ἔσῃ/ἔσει	εἴσῃ	**εἶ**	φήσεις
	3rd sing.	**ἔσται**	εἴσεται	**εἶσι(ν)**	φήσει
	1st pl.	ἐσόμεθα	εἰσόμεθα	**ἴμεν**	φήσομεν
	2nd pl.	ἔσεσθε	εἴσεσθε	**ἴτε**	φήσετε
	3rd pl.	ἔσονται	εἴσονται	**ἴασι(ν)**	φήσουσι(ν)
fut. opt.	**1st sing.**	ἐσοίμην etc.	εἰσοίμην etc.	—	φήσοιμι etc.
fut. part.	**nom. sing.**	ἐσόμενος	εἰσόμενος	—	φήσων
(§34, §26)		-η -ον	-η -ον		-ουσα -ον
fut. inf.		ἔσεσθαι	εἴσεσθαι	—	φήσειν

Dual Forms

§ 67 Dual endings for nouns, adjectives, and participles

- Dual endings are occasionally used instead of plural endings on nouns that are two in number or on adjectives or participles modifying two nouns.
- There is no real difference in translating these, although the word *two* may be inserted into the sentence modifying the noun, if desired.

	1st decl.	2nd decl.	3rd decl.
nom./acc./voc.	-α	-ω	-ε (-ει/-η with vowel stems)
gen./dat.	-αιν	-οιν	-οιν (-ῳν with some vowel stems)

§ 68 Dual forms of definite article, οὗτος, and first-person and second-person pronoun

- Dual forms of the definite article, the demonstrative adjective, and first- and second-person pronouns are occasionally used instead of plural forms to modify or replace nouns that are two in number.
- There is no real difference in translating these, although the word two may be inserted into the sentence modifying the noun or pronoun, if desired.

	def. art. (all genders)	οὗτος (all genders)	1st pers. pron. ("we two")	2nd pers. pron. ("you two")
nom./acc./voc.	τώ	τούτω	νώ	σφώ
gen./dat.	τοῖν	τούτοιν	νῷν	σφῷν

§ 69 Basic dual endings for verbs

- A dual ending is occasionally used instead of a plural when the subject of the verb is two in number. There is no real difference in translating, though the word two may be inserted into the sentence modifying the subject, if desired.
- Dual forms of verbs are formed using the same stem and augment as the corresponding plural forms of the same verb. Appropriate stems and augments are given in the verbs section of the grammar.

It is perhaps easiest to generate the dual forms by analogy, using the corresponding second-person plural of a given verb as a model and the charts below. For example, the present active indicative second-person plural of the regular verb λύω is λύετε, so the present active indicative second-person dual is λύετον, as is the third-person dual. The imperfect middle-passive indicative second-person plural of the contract verb φιλέω is ἐφιλεῖσθε, so the imperfect middle-passive indicative second-person dual is ἐφιλεῖσθον, and the third-person dual is ἐφιλείσθην. The aorist middle optative second-person plural of δείκνυμι is δείξαισθε, so the aorist middle optative second-person dual is δείξαισθον, and the third-person dual is δειξαίσθην. The present indicative second-person plural of εἰμί is ἐστέ so the present indicative second dual is ἐστόν, and so on.

Present, future, perfect active
- Sometimes the perfect is formed periphrastically (i.e., with a perfect participle + the appropriate form of εἰμί).

	indic.	impera.	subju.	opt.
2nd dual	-τον	-τον	-τον	-τον
3rd dual	-τον	-των	-τον	-την

Imperfect and pluperfect active indicative, aorist active and passive

	indic.	impera.	subju.	opt.
2nd dual	-τον	-τον	-τον	-τον
3rd dual	-την	-των	-τον	-την

Present, future, perfect middle and passive
- Sometimes the perfect is formed periphrastically (i.e., with a perfect participle + the appropriate form of εἰμί).

	indic.	impera.	subju.	opt.
2nd dual	-σθον	-σθον	-σθον	-σθον
3rd dual	-σθον	-σθων	-σθον	-σθην

Imperfect and pluperfect middle-passive indicative, aorist middle

	indic.	impera.	subju.	opt.
2nd dual	-σθον	-σθον	-σθον	-σθον
3rd dual	-σθην	-σθων	-σθον	-σθην

Numerals

§ 70 Greek number system

- Words in bold and suffixes should be memorized; the larger patterns should be noted. Missing numbers should be *recognizable* from studying the patterns but may be challenging to produce. For the spelling of missing numbers, many of which use the adverbial rather than the ordinal stem, see H. W. Smyth, *Greek Crammer*, 2nd ed., rev. by G. M. Messing (Cambridge: Harvard University Press, 1956), sect. 347 (347).
- Asterisked words (including adverbs) do not decline.

	cardinal	ordinal (§6)	adv.
1 (α΄)	εἷς μία ἕν (one)	πρῶτος -η -ον (first)	ἅπαξ* (once)
2 (β΄)	δύο	δεύτερος -α -ον	δίς*
3 (γ΄)	τρεῖς τρία	τρίτος -η -ον	τρίς*
4 (δ΄)	τέτταρες τέτταρα	τέταρτος -η -ον	τετράκις*
5 (ε΄)	πέντε*	πέμπτος -η -ον	πεντάκις*
6 (ϛ΄) [stigma]	ἕξ*	ἕκτος -η -ον	ἑξάκις*
7 (ζ΄)	ἑπτά*	ἕβδομος -η -ον	ἑπτάκις*
8 (η΄)	ὀκτώ*	ὄγδοος -η -ον	ὀκτάκις*
9 (θ΄)	ἐννέα*	ἔνατος -η -ον	ἐνάκις*
10 (ι΄)	δέκα*	δέκατος -η -ον	δεκάκις*
11 (ια΄)	ἕνδεκα*	ἑνδέκατος -η -ον	ἑνδεκάκις*
12 (ιβ΄)	δώδεκα*	δωδέκατος -η -ον	δωδεκάκις*
13 (ιγ΄)	τρισκαίδεκα* *or* τρεῖς καὶ δέκα	τρίτος καὶ δέκατος	τρισκαιδεκάκις*
14–19 (ιδ΄–ιθ΄)	—καὶ δέκα	—καὶ δέκατος	—καιδεκάκις*
20 (κ΄)	εἴκοσι(ν)*	εἰκοστός -ή -όν	εἰκοσάκις*
30 (λ΄)	τριάκοντα*	τριακοστός -ή -όν	τριακοσάκις*
40–90 (μ΄–ϙ΄)	-κοντα*	-κοστός -ή -όν	-κοσάκις*
100 (ρ΄)	ἑκατόν*	ἑκατοστός -ή -όν	ἑκατοσάκις*
200 (σ΄)	διάκοσιοι -αι -α	διακοσιοστός -ή -όν	διακοσιάκις*
300 (τ΄)	τριακόσιοι -αι -α	τριακοσιοστός -ή -όν	τριακοσιάκις*
400–900 (υ΄–ϡ΄)	-κόσιοι -αι -α	-κοσιοστός -ή -όν	-κοσιάκις*
1,000 (,α)	χίλιοι -αι -α	χιλιοστός -ή -όν	χιλιάκις*

§ 70 Greek number system (continued)

	cardinal	ordinal (§6)	adv.
2,000 (,β)	δισχίλιοι -αι -α	δισχιλιοστός -ή -όν	δισχιλιάκις*
3,000 (,γ)	τρισχίλιοι -αι -α	τρισχιλιοστός -ή -όν	τρισχιλιάκις*
4,000–9,000	**-χίλιοι -αι -α**	-χιλιοστός -ή -όν	-χιλιάκις*
10,000 (,ι)	**μύριοι -αι -α**	μυριοστός -ή -όν	μυριάκις*
20,000 (,κ)	δισμύριοι -αι -α	δισμυριοστός -ή -όν	δισμυριάκις*
30,000 (,λ)	τρισμύριοι -αι -α	τρισμυριοστός -ή -όν	τρισμυριάκις*
40,000–90,000	**-μύριοι -αι -α**	-μυριοστός -ή -όν	-μυριάκις*

§ 71 Numerals with irregular declensions

	one (εἷς μία ἕν)			two (δύο)
	masc.	**fem.**	**neut.**	**masc./fem./neut.**
nom.	εἷς	μία	ἕν	δύο
gen.	ἑνός	μιᾶς	ἑνός	δυοῖν
dat.	ἑνί	μιᾷ	ἑνί	δυοῖν
acc.	ἕνα	μίαν	ἕν	δύο

	three (τρεῖς τρία)		four (τέτταρες τέτταρα)	
	masc./fem.	**neut.**	**masc./fem.**	**neut.**
nom.	τρεῖς	τρία	τέτταρες	τέτταρα
gen.	τριῶν	τριῶν	τεττάρων	τεττάρων
dat.	τρισί(ν)	τρισί(ν)	τέτταρσι(ν)	τέτταρσι(ν)
acc.	τρεῖς	τρία	τέτταρας	τέτταρα

Part 2
Essentials of Greek Syntax

Nouns and Pronouns

Common uses of the nominative (§§72–75)

§ 72 Nominative subject of a finite verb

- in a main or dependent clause

πάντας ἐξαπατᾷ **αὕτη ἡ θεά**. = **This goddess** deceives everyone.
τίς βούλεται πυθέσθαι τοιαῦτα; = **Who** wishes to learn such things?
εἰπέ μοι πότε ἐγένετο **ἡ συνουσία αὕτη**. = Tell me when **this gathering** occurred.

§ 73 Predicate nominative

- with a linking verb (e.g., εἰμί, γίγνομαι, φαίνομαι) expressed or understood
- renaming or labeling the subject
- normally distinguished from the subject by the absence of the definite article

μετὰ δὲ τοῦτο **στρατηγὸς** ὁ Ἀλκιβιάδης ἐγένετο. = After this, Alcibiades became **general**.
ποιητὴς καλὸς οὔκ εἰμι. = I am not a good **poet**.
αὐτὸς **στρατηγὸς** ᾑρέθη. = He himself was chosen **general**. [note absence of definite article:"the general himself" = αὐτὸς ὁ στρατηγός]
φαίνεται μοι ἐκεῖνος **θεός**. = That man seems to me [to be] **a god**. [note absence of definite article:"that god" = ἐκεῖνος ὁ θεός]

- Forms of the verb εἰμί may be omitted in Greek, and the reader must supply the appropriate form of the verb "be" for good English sense.

δεινὸς **δαίμων** ὁ Ἔρως, ὡς οἶμαι. = Eros [is] an awesome **divinity**, as I think.
τότε δὲ **στρατηγὸς** ὁ Περικλῆς. = At that time Pericles [was] **general**.

§ 74 Nominative in apposition,[1] renaming the subject

ὑμεῖς **οἱ ποιηταὶ** ἀληθῆ οὐκ ἴστε. = You **poets** do not know the truth.

§ 75 Nominative in comparison[2] to the subject, after a comparative + ἤ

ἐν τῇ μάχῃ ὁ Σωκράτης ἀνδρειότερος ἦν ἢ **οἱ** τῶν Ἀθηναίων **στρατηγοί**.
= In the battle Socrates was braver than **the generals** of the Athenians.

Common uses of the accusative (§§76–88)

§ 76 Accusative as direct object of a transitive verb

τοὺς βαρβάρους οἱ Ἕλληνες ἐνίκησαν. = The Greeks beat **the barbarians**.

- Accusatives can be objects of nonfinite verbs (participles and infinitives).

  πολλὰ χρήματα ὀφείλων, ὁ γέρων **τὸν ἄδικον λόγον** μαθεῖν ἐβούλετο.
  = Owing **much money**, the old man wished to learn **the unjust argument**. *or* Since he owed **much money**, the old man wished to learn **the unjust argument**.

§ 77 Cognate accusative
- The accusative noun is closely related to the governing verb.

  θύσας **θυσίαν** τοῖς θεοῖς, ἐκεῖνος ἔβη εἰς τὴν πόλιν. = Having sacrificed **a sacrifice** to the gods, he went into the city. *or* Having performed **a sacrifice** to the gods, he went into the city.
  πολλὴν **φλυαρίαν** φλυαρεῖ ὁ Ἀριστοφάνης. = Aristophanes talks much **nonsense**. [φλυαρέω = talk nonsense]
  ὑπὲρ ἀθανασίας πολλοὺς **πόνους** πονοῦμεν καὶ μεγίστους **κινδύνους** κινδυνεύομεν. = For the sake of immortality we suffer many **toils** and risk the greatest **hazards**.

§ 78 Predicate accusative
- with certain verbs (e.g., ποιέω, καλέω, ἡγέομαι, νομίζω, αἱρέομαι)
- two accusatives: a direct object and predicate accusative
- predicate accusative usually distinguished from direct object because it does not have a definite article

---

1. Apposition can occur in any case (§120).
2. Comparison can occur in any case (§121).

ἐκεῖνοι ἐκάλουν ἡμᾶς **βαρβάρους**. = Those men called us **barbarians**.
βασιλέα ἐποιήσαμεν τοῦτον τὸν ἄνδρα. = We made this man **king**.

§ 79 Double accusative

- with certain verbs (e.g., διδάσκω, ἐρωτάω, ποιέω, λέγω)

Σωκράτης **τοὺς νεανίας** *πολλὰ* ἐδίδασκεν. = Socrates taught **the young men** *many things*.
πολλὰ ἀγαθὰ **ὑμᾶς** ἐποίησεν. = He did **you** *much good*.
ἡμᾶς *πολλά τε καὶ κακὰ* ἔλεγε. = He said *many bad things* [about] **us**.

§ 80 Accusative time phrase, to express duration

- supply relevant preposition in English

πολλὰς ἡμέρας ἐπορευόμεθα. = We traveled **for many days**.
ὀλίγον χρόνον καθευδήσομεν. = We will sleep **for a little while** [a small time].

- Note also related but rarer accusative of extent of space.

ἐννέα στάδια ἐβαίνομεν. = We walked **[for] nine stades**.

§ 81 Adverbial accusative

- Though more common with adjectives, nouns are occasionally used this way.

τίνα τρόπον πιόμεθα; = **In what way** will we drink?
τέλος δ᾽ ὡμολόγησα. = **At last**, I agreed. *or* **Finally**, I agreed.
τὸ μὲν ἄρρεν ἦν τοῦ ἡλίου **τὴν ἀρχὴν** ἔκγονον. = **In the beginning**, the male was the offspring of the sun. *or* **Originally**, the male was the offspring of the sun.

§ 82 Accusative of respect

- accompanies an adjective or verb to specify in what respect a description is true
- common with body parts
- supply relevant preposition in English

οὕτως εἶπε **ποδὰς** ὠκὺς Ἀχιλλεύς. = Thus spoke Achilles, swift **with respect to feet**. [swift-footed Achilles in Homer's *Iliad*]
τυφλὸς **τά τ᾽ ὦτα** τόν τε νοῦν **τά τ᾽ ὄμματ᾽** εἶ. = You are blind **in ears and mind and eyes**. [Teiresias, the blind prophet, to Oedipus in Sophocles' *Oedipus the King*]
καρδίαν πάσχω. = I suffer **in my heart**.

οὗτοι δεινοὶ **μάχην**. = These men [are] terrible **in battle**.
διαφέρει γυνὴ ἀνδρὸς **τὴν φύσιν**. = Woman differs from man **in nature**.
ἀγαθὸς μὲν **οὔ τι**, κακὸς δὲ **πάντα** εἶ. = You are good **in no way**, bad **in every way**.

§ 83 Accusative subject of infinitive

- in natural result clauses, πρίν-clauses, and articular infinitives
- when subject is different from subject of main verb

  οὕτως κακὸς ὁ στρατηγὸς ἦν ὥστε τὸν θάνατον **τοὺς στρατιώτας** φοβεῖσθαι.
  = The general was so bad that **the soldiers** feared death.
  πρὶν **τὸν Ἀλκιβιάδην** ἀφικέσθαι, οἱ ἑταῖροι περὶ τὸν Ἔρωτα διελέγοντο.
  = Before **Alcibiades** arrived, the companions were discussing Eros.
  διὰ τὸ **αὐτὸν** φλυαρεῖν οἱ φίλοι ἐγέλασαν. = On account of **him** talking nonsense the friends laughed. _or_ Because **he** talked nonsense, his friends laughed.

§ 84 Accusative subject of indirect statement with infinitive or participle

- when subject of indirect statement is different from subject of main verb

  οἶδα **πολλοὺς νεανίας** ὑπὸ τοῦ Σωκράτους διδαχθέντας. = I know that **many young men** have been taught by Socrates.
  οὔ φημι **ἡμᾶς** ἠδικηκέναι. = I deny that **we** have acted unjustly. _or_ I say that **we** have not acted unjustly.

§ 85 Accusative in many impersonal constructions

- with δεῖ, χρή, ἔστι + infinitive, etc.

  δεῖ **ὑμᾶς** λέγειν τὴν ἀλήθειαν. = It is necessary **for you** to speak the truth.
  ἀνάγκη ἦν **αὐτοὺς** ταῦτα μαθεῖν. = It was necessary **for them** to learn these things.
  οὐκ ἔστιν **πάντας** ὁμολογεῖν. = It is not possible **for all people** to agree.
  τὸν Ἔρωτα καὶ **ἡμᾶς** δίκαιον ἐπαινέσαι. = It is right **for us** too to praise Eros.

§ 86 Accusative with λανθάνω + supplementary participle

- translate: "_subject_ escapes the notice of _accusative_ in ——ing _or accusative_ does not notice _subject_ ——ing"

  ἔλαθες **με** ὁμολογῶν. = You escaped **my notice** in agreeing. _or_ I didn't notice you agreeing.

§ 87 Accusative object of prepositions

- particularly when motion "toward" or "along" is implied

αἱ νῆες παρὰ **τὴν νῆσον** ἐλθοῦσαι εἰς **τὸν λιμένα** ᾖσαν. = The ships, having gone beside **the island**, went into **the harbor**.

ἐπὶ **τοὺς βαρβάρους** ἡ στρατιὰ ἐπέρχεται. = The army advances against **the barbarians**.

§ 88 Accusative in oaths

- with μά or νή

μὰ Δία = by Zeus *or* no, by Zeus
νὴ τοὺς θεοὺς τοῦ οὐρανοῦ = by the gods of heaven *or* yes, by the gods of heaven

Common uses of the genitive (§§89–105)

Genitives used to modify nouns (§§89–92)

- translate: "of —— *or* for —— *or* ——'s" or similar
- may be broken down into smaller categories, as below

§ 89 Genitive of possession

- indicating possession, ownership, authorship, and most interpersonal relationships
- translate: "of —— *or* ——'s" or similar

ἡ οἰκία ἡ **Ἀγάθωνος** = **Agathon's** house
οἱ **Σωκράτους** λόγοι καὶ **τῶν ἄλλων** = the words **of Socrates and the others**
ἑταῖρος **Σωκράτους** = companion **of Socrates**
ἐραστὴς **Σωκράτους** = lover **of Socrates**
πατὴρ **ἀνδρῶν** τε **θεῶν** τε = father **of men and gods**
ἡ **Πελίου** θυγάτηρ Ἄλκηστις = Alcestis, the daughter **of Pelias**
οἱ **τῆς πόλεως** νόμοι = the laws **of the city**
οἱ **Σόλωνος** νόμοι = the laws **of Solon** [i.e., those he authored]
μαθητὴς **Ἔρωτος** = Eros's student, a student **of Eros**
ἡ **Εὐριπίδου** Μελανίππη = **Euripides'** Melanippe [i.e., the character he created]

- with the noun omitted and understood from context

Φοίνιξ **τοῦ Φιλίππου** = Phoinix **[son] of Philippos** [υἱός is *regularly* omitted]
Διὸς Ἄρτεμις = Artemis **[daughter] of Zeus**

Ἄλκηστις τοῦ Ἀδμήτου = Alcestis **[wife] of Admetus**
τὸ τοῦ Ὁμήρου = **Homer's** thing [i.e., Homer's maxim or Homer's line]
εἰς Ἀγάθωνος = to **Agathon's [house]**
ἐν Ἀγάθωνος = at **Agathon's [house]**
εἰς Ἅιδου = to **Hades' [house]**
ἐν Ἅιδου = in **Hades' [house]**

§ 90 Genitive of description

- giving material, contents, quality, or size of an object

  ὁ δ' Ἀλκιβιάδης εἶχεν **κιττοῦ** τέ τινα στέφανον **καὶ ἴων**. = Alcibiades had a crown **of ivy and violets**.

  ὁ δὲ **τοῦ ἤθους** χρηστοῦ ὄντος ἐραστὴς διὰ βίου μένει. = The lover [who is] **of a character** that is good remains throughout life. *or* The lover **characterized by a character** that is good remains throughout life.

§ 91 Subjective genitive

- With nouns that denote actions, the genitive can denote the subject of the action.

  ἡ **Πάριος** κρίσις = the judgment **of Paris** (i.e., **Paris** judged.)
  ἡ **τῆς θεᾶς** ἀπάτη = the **goddess's** deception (i.e., **The goddess** deceived.)

§ 92 Objective genitive

- With nouns that denote actions, the genitive can denote the object of the action.

  ἡ **Διὸς** ἀπάτη = the deception **of Zeus** (i.e., Hera deceived **Zeus**.)
  ἡ ἐπιθυμία **τοῦ πλούτου** = the desire **for wealth** (i.e., People desire **wealth**.)
  ὁ ἔρως **τοῦ κάλλους** = the love **of beauty** (i.e., People love **beauty**.)
  ἔρως Ἀφροδίτης Ἄρη ἔχει = love **of Aphrodite** holds [has a grip on] Ares. (i.e., Ares loves **Aphrodite**.)
  μαθητὴς **μουσικῆς** = a student **of the musical art** (i.e., He studies **the musical art**.)
  τὰς **τοῦ χειμῶνος** καρτερήσεις = his acts of endurance **of winter** *or* his toughness in **winter** (i.e., He endures **winter**.)

Genitives that do not modify nouns (§§93–105)

§ 93 Partitive genitive (genitive of the whole)

- common with a superlative, τις/τι, τίς/τί, and enumerative words (πολλοί, ὀλίγοι, numbers) μέγιστος **τῶν Ἑλλήνων φιλοσόφων** ἦν ὁ Σωκράτης. = Socrates was the greatest **of the Greek philosophers**.

τῶν φίλων τις ἰδών με ἐκάλεσεν. = One **of [my] friends** upon seeing me called [me].

τὴν ἀλήθειαν ἴσασιν **αὐτῶν** τινες. = Some **of them** know the truth.

τίς **ἡμῶν** οὕτω σοφὸς ὥστε ἀεὶ τὴν ἀλήθειαν εἰδέναι; = Who **of us** [is] so wise as to always know the truth? or Which **of us** [is] so wise as to always know the truth?

- also found with adverbs

  ποῦ **τῆς γῆς** ἐσμέν; = Where **on earth** are we? or In what part **of the earth** are we?

  ἐνταῦθα **τοῦ βίου** = at this point **in life** or at this stage **of life**

§ 94 Genitive of comparison (see also §121)
- with a comparative adjective or adverb
- translate: "than ——"

  τίς σοφώτερος ἦν **τοῦ Σωκράτους**; = Who was wiser **than Socrates**?

  κρείττων δὲ ὁ ἔχων **τοῦ ἐχομένου**. = The one who holds is stronger **than the one who is held**.

§ 95 Genitive of time within which
- in translating, supply an English preposition to express a general time frame within which events occur

  τῆς νυκτὸς ἡ στρατιὰ ἀφίκετο. = The army arrived **during the night**.

  νυκτὸς μὲν καθεύδω, **ἡμέρας** δὲ τὴν σοφίαν ζητῶ. = **During the night** [or **by night**], I sleep; **during the day** [or **by day**], I seek wisdom.

  ἑκάστης ἡμέρας σύνειμι Σωκράτει. = **Each day** I spend time with Socrates.

§ 96 Subject of a genitive absolute (see also §176)
- with participle agreeing in case, number, gender

  λέγοντος **σοῦ**, ὦ διδάσκαλε, ἐκαθεύδομεν. = While **you** were speaking, o teacher, we were sleeping.

§ 97 Genitive of value or price

  πόσου διδάσκει; **πέντε μνῶν**. = Q: **For how much** does he teach? A: **For five mnas**.[3]

---

3. A mna is a unit of money equivalent to 100 drachmas.

§ 98 Genitive of cause

- with verbs of emotion, the genitive gives the cause of the emotion

τοῦ πάθους ᾠκτίρομεν αὐτόν. = We pitied him **for his suffering**.

ἐθαύμασα **τῆς τόλμης** τῶν λεγόντων. = I wondered **at the daring** of the speakers.

τοῦτον ἄγαμαι **τῆς πραότητος**. = I admire this man **for his gentleness**.

ζηλῶ σε **τοῦ νοῦ, τῆς δὲ δειλίας** στυγῶ. = I envy you **for your intelligence**, but I hate [you] **for your cowardice**. [Sophocles, *Electra*]

τίς οὐκ ἂν ἐξεπλάγη **τοῦ κάλλους** τούτου τοῦ λόγου; = Who would not have been astonished **at the beauty** of this speech?

§ 99 Genitive of source

- accompanying ideas of birth and parentage

τῆς μὲν **Διώνης καὶ Διὸς** γίγνεται ἡ πάνδημος Ἀφροδίτης, **τοῦ** δ' **Οὐρανοῦ** ἡ οὐρανίη Ἀφροδίτη, οὖσα ἀμήτωρ. = **From Dione and Zeus** is born the popular Aphrodite, but **from Ouranos** [comes] the heavenly Aphrodite, who is motherless.

πατρὸς δὲ **τίνος** ἐστιν Ἔρως καὶ **μητρός**; = **From what father** and **mother** is Eros? *or* **From what father** and **mother** is Eros [born]?

§ 100 Genitive object of many verbs

οἱ τοιοῦτοι ἐρῶσι **γυναικῶν**. = Men of this kind have desire for **women**. *or* Men of this kind love **women**.

ὁ ἱκέτης ἐλάβετο **τοῦ βωμοῦ**. = The supplicant took hold of **the altar**. *or* The supplicant grasped **the altar**.

This genitive-verb relationship is normally indicated in the dictionary entry for that word. Common categories of verbs that take genitive objects are verbs of . . .

- sharing (e.g., μετέχω)
- separation (e.g., λήγω, χωρίζω)
- physical touching (e.g., λαμβάνομαι, ἅπτομαι)
- lacking, desiring, wanting, and needing (e.g., ἐράω, ἐπιθυμέω, δέομαι)
- remembering and forgetting (e.g., ἐπιλανθάνομαι, μέμνημαι, μιμνήσκομαι)
- ruling or surpassing (e.g., ἄρχω, περίειμι)
- filling and emptying (e.g., πληρόω, κενόω)
- with compounds of κατά implying negative judgment (καταδικάζω, καταφρονέω, καταγελάω)
- hearing or perceiving a person (e.g., ἀκούω, πυνθάνομαι)
  ἀκούω usually takes genitive of person heard + accusative of thing heard

ταῦτα **Σωκράτους αὐτοῦ** ἤκουσα. = I heard these things **from Socrates himself**.

αὐλητρίδος ἠκούσαμεν. = We heard **a flute girl** (i.e., the voice of a flute girl). [Cf. πολὺν ψόφον καὶ **αὐλητρίδος** φωνὴν ἠκούσαμεν. = We heard a loud noise and **a flute girl's** voice.]

§ 101 Genitive of separation

- Some verbs may take an accusative object together with a genitive of separation.

σῶσον ἡμᾶς **κακοῦ** = Save us **from evil**.

οἱ Ἀθηναῖοι ἐβούλοντο παῦσαι αὐτὸν **τῆς στρατηγίας**. = The Athenians wished to stop him **from his generalship**. [i.e., they wanted to remove him from his generalship]

§ 102 Genitive with certain adjectives

- particularly those expressing separation or lack, fullness, origin, or cause (e.g., αἴτιος, ἄξιος, ἐλεύθερος, κενός, πλέως, πλήρης)
- translate closely with the adjective

πλήρης αὕτη ἡ πόλις **τῶν τε ἀγαθῶν ποιητῶν καὶ τῶν κακῶν ῥητόρων**. = This city [is] full **of good poets and bad politicians**.

§ 103 Genitive object of prepositions

- particularly those expressing separation, origin, causation, or general vicinity (ἀπό, ἐκ, ἐγγύς, διά, ἐναντίον, ἐπί, μετά, περί, ὑπέρ, ὑπό, ἕνεκα)

ἄνδρα τινὰ ἐκ **τοῦ λιμένος** διὰ **τῆς ἀγορᾶς** ἐλθόντα εἴδομεν. = We saw a certain man coming from **the harbor** through **the agora**.

§ 104 Predicate genitive of characteristic

- with a linking verb expressed or implied, showing the person or thing whose nature, duty, custom, or the like it is to perform an action in the infinitive

τὸ μετρίως πίνειν οὐ **παντός**, ἀλλ᾽ **ἀνδρὸς σώφρονος**. = Drinking in moderation [is] **characteristic** not **of everyone** but **of the moderate man**. or **It is the moderate man**, not **everyone, who characteristically** drinks in moderation.

τοῦ αὐτοῦ ἀνδρός ἐστι κωμῳδίαν καὶ τραγῳδίαν ἐπίστασθαι ποιεῖν. = It is **characteristic of the same man** to know how to make comedy and tragedy. or **The same man characteristically** knows how to make comedy and tragedy.

§ 105 Genitive of exclamation

ὦ τῆς ἀνοίας, ὦ τῆς ὕβρεως. = Oh, **the folly! The hubris!**

Common uses of the dative (§§106–118)

§ 106 Dative as indirect object

- usually animate
- translate: "to —— or for ——"

ὑμῖν τὴν ἀλήθειαν λέγειν βούλομαι. = I wish to tell **you** the truth. or I wish to tell the truth **to you**.

τῇ θεᾷ τὰς θυσίας ἐθύσαμεν. = We made sacrifices **to the goddess**.

οἱ θεοὶ δοῖεν **μοι** τόδε. = May the gods grant **me** this.

§ 107 Dative of the possessor (dative of possession)

- animate
- usually accompanied by a nominative with some form of the verb "to be" either expressed or understood

σύ **μοι** [εἶ] πατὴρ καὶ πότνια μήτηρ. = You [are] father and revered mother **to me**. or You are **my** father and revered mother. [Andromache to Hektor in *Iliad* 6]

Οὖτις **ἐμοί** γ᾿ ὄνομα. = The name **to me** [is] No one. or **My** name is No one. [Odysseus to Cyclops in *Odyssey* 9]

§ 108 Dative of means

- inanimate
- translate: "by —— or with ——"

τοῖς μὲν **ὅπλοις** τὴν πόλιν ἐλάβομεν, **τοῖς** δὲ **λόγοις** τοὺς πολίτας ληψόμεθα. = **With weapons** we captured the city, **with words** we shall capture the citizens.

§ 109 Dative of manner

- inanimate, usually abstract noun
- translate: "with —— or ——ly or in ——"

τῷ **ὄντι** πάνυ χαλεπῶς ἔχω = **In fact**, I am altogether a mess. or **Actually**, I am doing very badly.

δικῇ καὶ **σοφίᾳ** ὁ φιλόσοφος εἶπεν. = The philosopher spoke **with justice** and **with wisdom**. or The philosopher spoke **justly** and **wisely**.

τῇ ἀληθείᾳ οὐδεὶς ἡμῶν οὐδὲν οἶδεν. = **In truth** none of us knows anything. or **Truly**, none of us knows anything.

§ 110　Dative of respect
- similar to accusative of respect (§82)
- related to dative of manner (§109)

ἀνὴρ **ἡλικίᾳ** ἔτι νέος = a man still young **in age** [i.e., young]
δυνατὸς μὲν **ἔργοις**, οὐ δὲ **λόγοις** = powerful **in deeds**, but not **in words**
κακὸς μὲν **τῷ σώματι**, καλὸς δὲ **τῇ ψυχῇ** = ugly **in body**, but beautiful **in soul**
λόγῳ μὲν σοφοὶ ἐκεῖνοι οἱ φιλόσοφοι, **ἔργῳ** δὲ μῶροί εἰσιν. = **In word** those philosophers are wise, but **in deed** they are foolish. *or* **By reputation** those philosophers are wise, but **in fact** they are foolish.

§ 111　Dative of degree of difference
- with a comparative or superlative adjective or adverb

ὀλίγῳ ἀμείνων = **a little** better *or* better **by a little**
δέκα ἡμέραις ὕστερον = **ten days** later *or* later **by ten days**
ἐκείνη ἡ ὁδὸς **πολλοῖς σταδίοις** μακροτέρα ἢ αὕτη. = That road is **many stades** longer than this one. [i.e., longer **by many stades**]

§ 112　Dative of time when
- to express point of time at which something occurs

ἐκείνῃ τῇ ἡμέρᾳ = on that day
τούτῳ τῷ χρόνῳ = at this time

§ 113　Ethical dative
- to indicate the interest of the speaker or to engage the interest of the audience
- almost exclusively first and second personal pronouns (μοι, σοι, ἡμῖν, ὑμῖν)

μέμνησθέ **μοι** μὴ θορυβεῖν. = Remember, **for my sake**, not to make a fuss. *or* **Please** remember not to get stirred up.
τοιοῦτον **ὑμῖν** ἐστι ἡ τυραννίς. = Tyranny is, **you know**, this sort of thing.

§ 114　Dative of personal agent
- with perfect passive or verbal adjective
- translate: "by ——"
- in other contexts, this idea is expressed by ὑπό + genitive
ταῦτα **τοῖς κακοῖς** πέπρακται. = These things have been done **by evil men**. *or* **Evil men** have done these things.
ὑμῖν αὕτη ἡ τεχνὴ μαθητέα. = This skill must be learned **by you**. *or* **You** must learn this skill. *or* It is necessary **for you** to learn this skill.

§ 115 Dative in impersonal constructions
- with, e.g., ἔξεστι or δοκεῖ (cf. §85)

οὐκ ἔξεστι **αὐτοῖς** πάντα ποιεῖν. = It is not possible **for them** to do everything.

§ 116 Dative with certain adjectives
- particularly those expressing similarity, friendliness, hostility; e.g., ὅμοιος, ἴσος, φίλος, ἐχθρός

Ὀδυσσεὺς λέγει πολλὰ ψεύδη **τῇ ἀληθείᾳ** ὁμοῖα. = Odysseus tells many lies resembling [similar to] **the truth**.

§ 117 Dative object of certain verbs
- Common verbs that use a dative object are πείθομαι (trust in, obey); ἕπομαι (follow); ἡγέομαι (lead); χράομαι (use, employ); ἐμπίπτω (fall upon, attack); ἐντυγχάνω (meet with).
- translate closely with the verb

οὐ πείσομαι **αὐτῷ**, κακῷ ἡγεμόνι ὄντι, ἀλλ᾽ ἕψομαι **τοῖς ἀμείνοσιν ἡγεμόσι.** = I will not obey **him**, since he is a bad leader, but I will follow **the better leaders**.

§ 118 Dative object of certain prepositions
- Usually when no movement to or away from is implied, the dative *fixes* the time and place.

κακοδαιμονέστατοι οἱ ἐν **τῇ πόλει** ἦσαν. = The people in **the city** were most unfortunate.

Common uses of the vocative (§119)

§ 119 Vocative of direct address
- used only to address people, gods, or (occasionally) things
- usually accompanied by ὦ
- never accompanied by definite article
- many of the forms (all plural, in fact) identical to the nominative

διὰ τί, ὦ **Σώκρατες**, ταῦτα ἐποίησας; = Why did you do these things, **Socrates**?

ἀκούετέ μου, ὦ **μέγιστοι**. = Hear me, **greatest [ones]**.

ὦ **χείρ**, τύπτε τὴν κακὴν γυναῖκα. = **Hand**, strike the evil woman!

Uses shared by all cases (§120–121)

§ 120 Apposition

- A noun or pronoun *in any case* may be accompanied by another noun or pronoun *in the same case* explaining, describing, or renaming the first; the second noun or pronoun is said to be in apposition to the first.

Σωκράτης **ὁ μέγας φιλόσοφος** οὐδὲν ᾔδει. = Socrates, **the great philosopher**, knew nothing.

ἄκουε ἡμῶν **τῶν κακοδαιμόνων ἱκέτων**. = Hear us [who are your] **miserable suppliants**.

τῷ ἡμετέρῳ πατρί, **τῷ βασιλεῖ**, ταῦτα εἰπέ. = Tell these things to our father, **the king**.

αὐτός τε ἄχθομαι ὑμᾶς τε **τοὺς ἑταίρους** ἐλεῶ. = I myself am annoyed, and I pity you, **my companions**.

ἄκουέ μου, ὦ Ζεῦ, **πάτερ** ἀνθρώπων καὶ θεῶν. = Hear me, Zeus, **father** of men and gods.

§ 121 Case use in comparisons

- There are two ways to make comparisons in Greek: (1) with a genitive of comparison (§94) or (2) with ἤ (than). When ἤ is used, the two things being compared are in the same case.

ὁ ἀνήρ ἐστι σοφώτερος ἢ **ὁ παῖς**. = **The man** is wiser than **the boy**.

οὗτος ὁ γέρων μωρότερός ἐστιν ἢ **ὁ υἱός**. = **This old man** is more foolish than **his son**.

μισῶ **τὸν γέροντα** μωρότερον ὄντα ἢ **τὸν υἱόν**. = I hate **the old man** who is more foolish than **his son**. *or* I hate **the old man**, since he is more foolish than **his son**.

Adjectives

Three basic uses of the adjective (§§122–124)

§ 122 Attributive use of the adjective; e.g., the *beautiful* ship, a *wise* man

- modifying a noun with which it agrees in case, number, and gender
- distinguished from predicate use (§123) by its position immediately following the definite article
- the three attributive positions:
  - ≈ between the definite article and the noun with which it agrees (like English)

πλέομεν ἐν τῇ **καλῇ** θαλάττῃ. = We are sailing on the **beautiful** sea.

οἱ **κακοὶ** ναῦται φεύγουσιν ἐκ τῶν **ἀγαθῶν** ἀνθρώπων. = The **bad** sailors are fleeing from the **good** men.

  - ≈ after the definite article repeated after the noun, with the adjective appended almost as an afterthought

ἐν τῇ θαλάττῃ τῇ **καλῇ** = on the **beautiful** sea [literally, on the sea, the **beautiful** one]

οἱ ναῦται οἱ **κακοί** = the **bad** sailors [literally, the sailors, the **bad** ones]

  - ≈ occasionally with the first definite article omitted

ἐν θαλάττῃ τῇ **καλῇ** = on the **beautiful** sea

ἐκ ἀνθρώπων τῶν **ἀγαθῶν** = from the **good** men

§ 123 Predicate use of the adjective; e.g., the ship is *beautiful*, the woman was *wise*

- with a linking verb (e.g., εἰμί, γίγνομαι, φαίνομαι, καλοῦμαι) expressed or understood

ἡ θεὰ **καλλίων** ἐγένετο. = The goddess became **more beautiful**.

σοφὴ οὔκ εἰμι. = I am not **wise**.

δεινὸς φαίνῃ. = You seem **clever**.

- Predicate position: since the linking verb can be omitted in Greek, the position of the adjective may be important in helping to distinguish predicate use from attributive use (§122); in predicate use the adjective does not directly follow the definite article.

καλὴ ἡ θάλαττα. = The sea [is] **beautiful**.
ἡ θάλαττα καλή. = The sea [is] **beautiful**.

- Predicate adjectives can occur in cases other than the nominative; again, the position of the adjective (not following the definite article) shows that it is predicate.

τὴν θάλατταν καλὴν ἡγοῦμαι. = I consider the sea **beautiful**.
ὁ θεὸς εὐδαίμονας ἐποίησε τοὺς πολίτας. = The god made the citizens **blessed**.

- An adjective in the predicate position may be used where English uses an adverb.

ἥσυχος καθεύδει ὁ κυβερνήτης. = The captain, **peaceful**, sleeps. *or* The captain sleeps **peacefully**.

- Demonstrative adjectives (οὗτος, ἐκεῖνος, ὅδε) are an exception; when used attributively they are placed in the predicate position.

ὅδε ὁ ναύτης λέγει. = **This** sailor is speaking.
ταύτην τὴν πόλιν μισῶ. = I hate **this** city.
βαῖνε εἰς τὸ πλοῖον ἐκεῖνο. = Go onto **that** ship.

§ 124 Substantive use of the adjective; e.g., I seek the *good*. The *wise* prevail.

- performs the function of a noun
- The adjective is used with a definite article or by itself, but without a noun.
- The gender and number of the adjective permit *inference* of the missing noun. (Remember that Greek uses many more substantives than English, so that it is often necessary to supply the missing noun for good sense in English.)

πολλὰ μὲν περὶ τῶν Ἀθηναίων ἴσμεν, ὀλίγα δὲ περὶ Λακεδαιμονίων. = We know **many things** about the Athenians, **few** about the Spartans.
ἐκεῖνος ταχέως διὰ τῆς ἀγορᾶς εἰς τὸν λιμένα ἔδραμεν. = **That man** ran swiftly through the agora into the harbor.
αὗται ἀεὶ πρὸς τοὺς νέους παίζουσιν, μῶρα λέγουσαι. = **These women** always tease **the young**, saying **foolish things**.
οὐκ οἶδεν οὐδεὶς οὐδέν. = **No one** knows **anything**.

Verbal adjectives (§§125–128)

§ 125 Verbal adjectives in -τέος

- adjective formed from verbal stems (but distinct from participle)
- carry idea of necessity (similar to Latin gerundive)
- two distinct uses: personal (§126) and impersonal (§127)

	modifying a noun or pronoun (§126)	neuter used impersonally (§127)
ἀκουστέος -α -ον from ἀκούω	to be heard, must be heard	one must hear
ἰτέος -α -ον from εἶμι	to be traveled, must be traveled	one must go
πειστέος -α -ον from πείθω	to be persuaded, must be persuaded	one must persuade
ποτέος -α -ον from πίνω	to be drunk, must be drunk	one must drink

§ 126 Personal (passive) construction of verbal adjectives in -τέος

- used as an adjective describing some noun or pronoun, with passive force: "to be ——ed *or* must be ——ed"
- indicates that the verbal action is *obligatory* and must be performed upon that noun or pronoun
- usually serves as a predicate adjective linked by the verb εἰμί to the noun or pronoun with which it agrees (compare passive periphrastic in Latin)

  πειστέοι οἱ ἄνδρες εἰσιν. = The men are **to be persuaded**. *or* The men **must be persuaded**.

- If the agent of the action is mentioned, the dative of personal agent (rather than ὑπό + genitive) is used.

  ὑμῖν οὗτοι λυτέοι εἰσιν. = These men are to be released **by you**. *or* **You** must release the men.

- When negated by οὐ the action must not occur.

  οὐκ ἀδικητέοι ἡμῖν εἰσιν οὗτοι. = These men **are not to be treated unjustly** by us. *or* We **must not treat** these men **unjustly**.

§ 127 Impersonal neuter (active) construction of verbal adjectives in -τέος

- used in the neuter nominative (usually singular), standing by itself (not modifying any noun or pronoun), may be accompanied by ἐστί, or ἐστί may be left unexpressed

- translate: "it is necessary for *accusative or dative* to *perform action of the verb* [with the adjective in -τεος given active force] *or accusative or dative* must *perform action of the verb*"

  ὑμᾶς **πολεμητέον ἐστι**. = **It is necessary** for you **to fight**. *or* You **must fight**.
  ἡμῖν **ποιητέον [ἐστι]** ταῦτα. = **It is necessary** for us **to do** these things. *or* We **must do** these things.

§ 128 Verbal adjectives in -τός
- adjective formed from verbal stems but distinct from participle
- carry two senses: capacity and achievement

	capacity	achievement
ἀκουστός -ή -όν **from** ἀκούω	capable of being heard, audible	heard
ἐρατός -ή -όν **from** ἐράω	capable of being loved, lovable, desirable	loved, desired
ὁρατός -ή -όν **from** ὁράω	capable of being seen, visible	seen

- Like verbal adjectives in -τέος, verbal adjectives in -τός may be accompanied by a dative of agent.

  τοῖς οἴκοι ζηλωτός = envied **by those** at home
  πολλοῖς ἐράτη = loved **by many**

Relative clauses (§§129–135)

§ 129 Relative clause and antecedent: basic definitions
Relative clause acts as an adjective to describe a noun or pronoun in the main clause of the sentence.

The grammatical term for a noun or pronoun modified by a relative clause is *antecedent*.

The antecedent may be expressed or simply inferred from the gender and number of the relative pronoun or adjective (§131).

Relative clause can be introduced by a relative pronoun (ὅς ἥ ὅ), an indefinite relative pronoun (ὅστις ἥτις ὅ τι), an intensified relative pronoun (ὅσπερ ἥπερ ὅπερ), or a relative adjective (οἷος -α -ον or ὅσος -η -ον).

§ 130 Normal agreement of relative pronouns or adjectives in relative clauses
- Relative pronouns and adjectives agree in gender and number with their antecedent; the case tells the function of the relative pronoun or adjective within the relative clause (following rules of case use; §§72–121).

οὐ γὰρ ἐγὼ ἀποφήσω, **ὃς** οὐδέν φημι ἄλλο ἐπίστασθαι ἢ τὰ ἐρωτικά. = For I, **who** claim to know nothing other than erotic matters, will not speak against [the proposal]. [nominative masculine singular relative pronoun ὃς agrees with masculine singular antecedent ἐγὼ and serves as the subject of the relative clause]

οὐδὲ μὴν ἀποφήσει Ἀριστοφάνης, **ᾧ** περὶ Διόνυσον καὶ Ἀφροδίτην πᾶσα ἡ διατριβή. = Nor indeed will Aristophanes, **whose** [dative of possession] entire way of life concerns Dionysus and Aphrodite, speak against [the proposal]. [dative masculine singular relative pronoun ᾧ agrees with masculine singular antecedent Ἀριστοφάνης and serves as dative of possession in a relative clause]

αὕτη ἐστὶν ἡ γυνὴ **ἣν** χθὲς ἐζητεῖτε. = This is the woman **whom** you were seeking yesterday. [accusative feminine singular relative pronoun ἣν agrees with feminine singular antecedent ἡ γυνὴ and serves as direct object of the relative clause]

πάντων **ἃ** ἕκαστος εἶπεν οὐ μέμνημαι. = I do not remember everything **which** [or **that**] each man said. [accusative neuter plural relative pronoun ἃ agrees with neuter plural antecedent πάντων and serves as direct object of a relative clause] [μέμνημαι takes genitive object]

§ 131 Suppressed antecedent/substantival relative clauses

- It is very common in Greek for the antecedent to be omitted and supplied from the gender and number of the relative pronoun or adjective; in this case, the relative clause acts like a substantival adjective, that is, like a noun.

ὅστις τῶν Μουσῶν ἐπιλανθάνεται, βίον διαφθείρει. = **Whoever** [or **he who**] forgets the Muses destroys life. [relative clause acts as subject of the sentence] [Sophocles]

ὅπερ ἐδεόμεθά σου ἡμῖν νῦν εἰπέ. = Now tell us **the very thing [which/ that]** we asked you. or Now tell us **exactly what** we asked you. [relative clause is direct object of the sentence]

οὐκ ἀμελετήτως ἔχω, **ὅπερ** ἀρχόμενος εἶπον. = I am not unpracticed, **the very thing which/that** I said as I began. or I am not unpracticed, **exactly what** I said as I began. [relative clause in apposition to the main clause of the sentence]

μοι Σωκράτης ἐνέτυχε λελουμένος τε καὶ τὰς βλαύτας ὑποδεδεμένος, **ἃ** ἐκεῖνος ὀλιγάκις ἐποίει. = Socrates met me, having bathed and put on sandals, **things which/that** he seldom did. [relative clause is in apposition to actions in main clause]

§ 132   Attraction of relative pronoun

- Attraction of the relative pronoun to the case of its antecedent is also common, thus violating the rules of normal agreement; this happens especially when the antecedent is a genitive or dative plural.

ἄλλος οὐδεὶς ἀποφήσει τουτωνὶ **ὧν** [instead of **οὖς**] ἐγὼ ὁρῶ. = No one else of these here **whom** I see will speak against [the proposal].

Μήδων **ὅσων**[1] [instead of **ὅσους**] ἑώρακα ὁ ἐμὸς πάππος κάλλιστος. = My grandfather is the most handsome of **all** the **many** Medes **whom** I have seen. *or* Of the Medes **as many as** I have seen my grandfather is the most handsome.

§ 133   Combination of suppressed antecedent (§131) and attraction (§132)

Δοκῶ μοι οὐκ ἀμελέτητος εἶναι περὶ **ὧν** [instead of **ἐκείνων ἃ**] πυνθάνεσθε. = I seem to myself to be not unpracticed concerning **those things about which** you ask. [cf. English: "concerning **what** you ask"]

Σωκράτη γε ἔνια ἤδη ἠρόμην **ὧν** [instead of **ἐκείνων ἃ**] ἐκείνου ἤκουσα. = I already asked Socrates, at any rate, about some **of those things** which/that I heard from that man. [cf. English: "about some **of what** I heard"]

§ 134   Moods in relative clauses

- Relative clauses may use moods other than the indicative, following the principles of conditional clauses (§164); particularly common are subjunctive + ἄν (generalizing primary sequence) and optative (no ἄν) (generalizing secondary sequence); for more examples, see §160, §152, and §159a.

ἐπιμελὲς πεποίημαι ἑκάστης ἡμέρας εἰδέναι **ὅ τι ἂν λέγῃ ἢ πράττῃ**. = I have made it my practice each day to know **whatever he says and does**. [subjunctive + ἄν in a relative clause: generalizing-primary sequence]

διέφθειρον πάντας **ὅσους λάβοιεν**. = They destroyed all **those many whom** they captured. [optative in a relative clause: generalizing-secondary sequence]

ὅντινα δὲ τέμοι, τὸν Ἀπόλλω ἐκέλευεν τὸ πρόσωπον μεταστρέφειν πρὸς τὴν τομήν. = **Whomever he cut**, he ordered Apollo to turn around his face toward the cut. *or* He ordered Apollo to turn the face of **whomever he cut** toward the cut. [optative in a relative clause: generalizing-secondary sequence]

---

1. For relative adjectives, see §135.

§ 135 Relative adjectives (οἷος -α -ον and ὅσος -η -ον) and their correlative demonstrative adjectives (τοιοῦτος -αύτη -οῦτο[ν] and τοσοῦτος -αύτη -οῦτο[ν]) in relative clauses

	quality	size/quantity
demonstrative ** οὗτος αὕτη** **τοῦτο (this, that)**	τοιοῦτος τοιαύτη τοιοῦτο (of this kind, of such a kind, such as this)	τοσοῦτος τοσαύτη τοσοῦτο (of this size, of this quantity, so much, so many)
relative ὅς ἥ ὅ **(who, which, that)**	οἷος -α -ον (of which kind, such as)	ὅσος -α -ον (of which size, of which number, as much as, as many as)

In relative clauses, the relative adjectives οἷος and ὅσος correspond to and function similarly to the relative pronoun ὅς ἥ ὅ, but οἷος suggests quality, ὅσος size or, in the plural, quantity.

The demonstrative adjectives τοιοῦτος and τοσοῦτος correspond to and function similarly to the demonstrative adjective οὗτος; τοιοῦτος suggests quality, τοσοῦτος size or, in the plural, quantity.

When the correlative pairs τοιοῦτος and οἷος *or* τοσοῦτος and ὅσος appear together, the relationship is similar to that between demonstrative and relative pronoun, but in the first case similarity of *quality* (type, kind) is being stressed, in the second similarity in *size* or *quantity* (usually a lot).

Frequently each individual relative adjective is not given its full translation; this is particularly true when it occurs with the corresponding demonstrative, because the meanings of the correlatives overlap considerably. The student should work to grasp the essential grammatical relationship and use the closest English idiom.

οὐ μέμνημαι πάντων **ὅσα** ἕκαστος εἶπεν. = I do not remember all **the many things which/that** each said. [the only difference between regular relative pronoun ἅ and relative adjective ὅσα here is that ὅσα emphasizes quantity]

μέμνημαι **τοιούτων οἷα** ἕκαστος εἶπεν. = I remember **the sorts of things which/that** each said. [the meanings of the correlatives τοιούτων and οἷα overlap, and the resulting translation is consequently much simpler than the translation of each word individually would suggest; the only difference between regular relative pronoun ἅ and relative adjective οἷα here is that οἷα emphasizes quality or kind; compare the use of regular demonstrative τούτων and the intensifying relative pronoun in this sentence: μέμνημαι τούτων ἅπερ ἕκαστος εἶπεν. = I remember **the exact things which/that** each said.]

ὑπὲρ ἀρετῆς ἀθανάτου πάντες πάντα ποιοῦσιν, **ὅσῳ** ἂν ἀμείνους ὦσι, **τοσούτῳ** μᾶλλον. = All people do everything for the sake of immortal excellence, **by which degree** they are better, **by that degree** they [do this] more. *or idiomatically* = All people do everything for the sake of immortal excellence; **the** better they are, **the** more they [do this]. [dative neuter singular relative adjective ὅσῳ agrees with dative singular antecedent τοσούτῳ and serves as dative of degree of difference in relative clause]

τὸ κόσμιον τοῦ σώματος ἐπιθυμεῖ **τοιούτων** ψόφων **οἷον** καὶ ὁ πταρμός ἐστιν. = The orderly part of the body desires **the sorts of** noises **such as** [*or* **of the kind that**] sneezing is in fact. [nominative neuter singular relative adjective οἷον serves as the subject complement of relative clause; singular οἷον is surprising with the plural antecedent τοιούτων ψόφων but is caused by sneezing being a single example of that kind of noise]

Verbs: Finite

A finite verb is a verb with person and number. Nonfinite verbs are the participle and infinitive.

§ 136 Person and number

- Person (first, second, third) and number (singular, dual, plural) of a verb match the verb's subject, with one exception: a neuter plural subject normally uses a singular verb.
- The subject can be omitted in Greek if it can be inferred from the verb ending.

verb	subject
1st sing.	I
2nd sing.	you
3rd sing.	he, she, it; *or* any singular noun, pronoun, or substantive*
1st pl.	we
2nd pl.	you (all)
3rd pl.	they; *or* any plural nominative noun, pronoun, or substantive (except neuter plural, which accompanies third singular)

*Neuter plural subjects also use third-person singular verbs.

A verb can be dual in number when the subject is composed of two people or things (§69). The translation of the verb may or may not reflect this.

ἐπεὶ δὲ τὼ θεὰ δύο **ἐστόν**, ἀνάγκη καὶ δύο Ἔρωτε εἶναι. = Since the goddesses **are** two, it is necessary that there be also two Erotes. [translation is not affected by verb form]

φυλακτέον ἑκάτερον τὸν ἔρωτα· **ἔνεστον** γάρ πᾶσι. = It is necessary to watch out for each of the two loves. For **the two** [*or* **both**] **are in** everything. [it is useful though not essential to reflect the dual verb form by adding "the two" or "both" for clarity]

§ 137 Voice: active, middle, passive

voice	action	translation of παύω (stop)
active	subject performs the action of the verb	I stop —— [I act on someone *or* something else]
passive	subject receives the action of the verb	I am stopped [I am acted upon by someone *or* something else]
middle	subject acts upon his/her/its/their self, acts in own interest or on behalf of self, or on something or someone belonging to self	I stop myself [I act on myself] [reflexive meaning]

Since the exact translation of a middle verb is not always easy to predict, dictionaries commonly list a distinct meaning for the middle, for example: "πείθω (persuade), *middle*: believe, obey, trust"—which yields:

active = I persuade [someone else]
passive = I am persuaded [by someone else]
middle = I believe, I obey

§ 138 Deponent verbs

A deponent verb always appears in middle or passive forms, but is translated actively. A middle deponent uses middle forms in the aorist; a passive deponent uses passive forms in the aorist. Deponents can be recognized by their dictionary entries: four (or fewer) principal parts, all of which have middle or passive endings. Middle deponents list the aorist in the third position, before the perfect; passive deponents list the aorist in the last position (i.e., in the aorist passive position), for example:

middle deponent: ἀφικνέομαι ἀφίξομαι **ἀφικόμην** ἀφῖγμαι: arrive (at)
passive deponent: βούλομαι βουλήσομαι βεβούλημαι **ἐβουλήθην**: wish; thus, ἐβουλήθην = I wished [active translation despite the passive form]

§ 139 Semideponent verbs

- Semideponent or partially deponent verbs use middle or passive forms with active translations in some (but not all) tenses; this can be inferred from the verb's principal parts.

  ἔρχομαι εἶμι/ἐλεύσομαι ἦλθον ἐλήλυθα: **go, come**[5]

- It is particularly common for verbs to be deponent only in the future.

  ἀκούω ἀκούσομαι ἤκουσα ἀκήκοα — ἠκούσθην: **hear**

---

5. Ἔρχομαι is deponent only in the present and in the future when εἶμι is not used.

Mood: indicative, imperative, subjunctive, optative (§§140–159)

Indicative mood (§§140–145)

§ 140 Indicative mood: normal uses of the tenses in statements, questions, and many dependent clauses

- negative οὐ (rare with μή = cautious assertion or a question expecting the answer "yes")
- present tense: present time, ongoing or repeated aspect

  νῦν ἀληθῆ λέγω. = **I am speaking** truthfully now. [ongoing aspect]
  ἀεὶ ἀληθῆ λέγω. = I always **speak** truthfully. [repeated aspect]

- imperfect tense: past time, ongoing or repeated aspect

  ἀληθῆ σοι ἔλεγον. = **I was telling** you the truth. [ongoing aspect]
  ἀεὶ ἀληθῆ ἔλεγον. = I always **used to speak** truthfully. [repeated aspect]

- future tense: future time, simple, repeated, or ongoing aspect

  αὔριον σοι ἐρῶ. = Tomorrow **I will tell** you. [simple aspect]
  ἀεὶ ἀληθῆ ἐρῶ. = **I will** always **speak** the truth. [repeated aspect]

- aorist tense: past time, simple aspect

  ἀληθῆ **εἶπον**. = **I spoke** truthfully.

- perfect tense: present time, completed aspect

  ἐδήδοκα πάντα τὸν σῖτον. = **I have eaten** all the food.

- pluperfect tense: past time, completed aspect

  ἠδηδόκη πάντα τὸν σῖτον. = **I had eaten** all the food.

- future perfect tense: future time, completed aspect

  ἐδηδοκυῖα ἔσομαι πάντα τὸν σῖτον. = **I will have eaten** all the food.

§ 141 Imperfect and aorist indicative in contrary-to-fact conditions (with ἄν) (§ 162) or (rare) in unattainable contrary-to-fact wishes (usually with εἰ γάρ or εἴθε)

- imperfect indicative = contrary-to-fact present
- aorist indicative = contrary-to-fact past

  εἰ οἱ πολῖται **ἦσαν** βελτίονες, ἡ πόλις κρείττων **ἦν ἄν**. = If the citizens **were** better, the city **would be** stronger. [present contrary-to-fact condition]
  εἰ γὰρ οἱ πολῖται **ἦσαν** βελτίονες. = If only the citizens **were** better! [present contrary-to-fact wish]

εἰ οἱ ἡμέτεροι στρατηγοὶ **ἐγένοντο** δεινότεροι, **ἐνικήσαμεν ἄν**. = If our generals **had been** cleverer, we **would have won**. [past contrary-to-fact condition]

εἴθ᾽ οἱ ἡμέτεροι στρατηγοὶ **ἐγένοντο** δεινότεροι. = If only our generals **had been** cleverer! [past contrary-to-fact wish]

§ 142 Ὅπως + future indicative: "see to it that ——"

ὅπως ταχέως **φεύξεσθε**. = **See to it that you flee** swiftly.

§ 143 Οὐ μή + future indicative: emphatic denial or urgent prohibition

οὐ μὴ φεύξεσθε = you won't flee [i.e., you can be sure of that!] *or* don't flee! [i.e., don't even think about it!]

§ 144 Ingressive aorist

- With a verb denoting a mental state or emotion or another state, the aorist often signals the initiation of that emotion or mental state; for example, ἐδάκρυε (imperfect indicative) = "he was weeping," but ἐδάκρυσε (aorist indicative) = "he burst into tears."

§ 145 Gnomic aorist (rare)

- Aorist indicative may occasionally be used to express a general truth and may be translated as present indicative.[6]

ἐπειδὰν ταῦτα, τά τε θερμὰ καὶ τὰ ψυχρὰ καὶ ξηρὰ καὶ ὑγρά, καὶ ἁρμονίαν καὶ κρᾶσιν λάβῃ σώφρονα, ἥκει φέροντα ὑγίειαν ἀνθρώποις καὶ τοῖς ἄλλοις ζῴοις τε καὶ φυτοῖς, καὶ οὐδὲν **ἠδίκησεν**. = Whenever these things—the hot and the cold and the dry and the wet—find a harmony and a mixture [that is] balanced, they come bringing health to men and to the other animals and plants, and **they do no harm**.

Imperative mood (§146)

§ 146 Imperative mood to issue direct commands

- negative μή
- occurs in present, aorist, and (very rarely and for only some verbs) perfect
- has only aspect, not tense
- second-person imperative

---

6. For further examples, see H. W. Smyth, *Greek Grammar*, 2nd ed. rev. by G. M. Messing (Cambridge: Harvard University Press, 1956), §1931.

εἰπέ μοι, ὦ θεά. = **Tell** me, goddess.

γνῶθι σεαυτόν. = **Know** yourself.

- third-person imperative

ὁ ξένος **εἰπέτω** τὸ ὄνομα. = **Let** the stranger **speak** his name.

[οἱ ἑταῖροι] **δησάντων** σ᾽ ἐν νηὶ θοῇ. = **Have** your companions **bind** you in the swift ship. [Circe's advice to Odysseus about resisting the Sirens in *Odyssey* 12]

Subjunctive mood (§§147–154)

Subjunctive mood: three common independent uses (§§147–149)

§ 147 Hortatory subjunctive

- first person (usually plural)
- translate: "let us/me ——"
- negative μή

μαχώμεθα = **let us fight**

μὴ **νικηθῶμεν** = **let us** not **be defeated** [passive]

§ 148 Deliberative subjunctive

- in a question (usually first person)
- translate: question word + "are we/am I to ——?"
- negative μή

τί **ποιῶμεν**; = What **are we to do**? *or* What **should we do**?

ποῖ **τρέπωμαι**; = Where **am I to turn**? *or* Where **should I turn**?

τί **ποιησθῇ**; = What **is to be done**? *or* What **should be done**? [third-person passive]

§ 149 Prohibitive subjunctive

- aorist second or (more rarely) third person
- always preceded by μή

μὴ θαυμάσητε. = **Don't wonder.** *or* **Don't be amazed.**

ὁ παῖς **μὴ βλαφθῇ.** = **Let** the child **not be harmed.** *or* **Don't let** the child **be harmed.** [passive]

ὅπερ ἄρτι ἐδεόμεθά σου, **μὴ** ἄλλως **ποιήσῃς.** = **Don't do** otherwise [than] precisely what I asked of you just now.

Subjunctive mood: two additional independent uses (relatively rare
(§§150–151)

§ 150 Subjunctive with μή in cautious assertion; μή οὐ in cautious denial (rare)

μὴ τοιοῦτος ᾖ. = **He is** that sort of man (**I suspect**).

μὴ οὐ τοιοῦτος ᾖ. = **He is not** that sort of man (**I don't think**).

ἀλλὰ **μὴ οὐ** τοῦτ' ᾖ χαλεπόν, ὦ ἄνδρες, θάνατον ἐκφυγεῖν. = But this—
fleeing death—is not difficult (I don't think), men. [Socrates, *Apology*]

μεθύοντα δὲ ἄνδρα παρὰ νηφόντων λόγους παραβάλλειν **μὴ οὐκ** ἐξ
ἴσου ᾖ. = **It would not be possible (I don't think)** for a drunk man to
compete on an even level against the words of sober people.

§ 151 Subjunctive with οὐ μή in urgent prohibition or emphatic denial (rare)

οὐ μὴ φύγητε. = **Don't you dare flee!** *or* **You wouldn't flee. (I'm con-
fident of that!)**

οὐ μὴ τοιοῦτος ᾖ. = **He is certainly not** that sort of man.

οὐ μὴ **παύσωμαι** φιλοσοφῶν. = **I certainly won't stop** philosophizing.
[Socrates, *Apology*]

τοσοῦτον ἐκπιὼν **οὐδὲν** μᾶλλον **μή** ποτε **μεθυσθῇ**. = Although drinking so
much, **he most emphatically does not** ever **become any** more **drunk**!

Subjunctive mood: three common dependent uses (i.e., in dependent
clauses) (§§152–154)

§ 152 Subjunctive with ἄν in a conditional, relative, or temporal clause (see
also §160)

- used to generalize or to express an indefinite time frame in the present or
future
- translate: "if [ever], whenever, whoever, until," etc. + present indicative
- negative μή

θαυμάζω ὅταν [=ὅτε ἄν] **ἴδω** τὴν πόλιν. = I am amazed whenever **I see**
the city.

ἴθι ὅποι **βούλῃ** ἄν. = Go wherever **you wish**.

ἐπιμελὲς πεποίημαι ἑκάστης ἡμέρας εἰδέναι ὅ τι ἄν **λέγῃ ἢ πράττῃ**. = I
have made it my practice each day to know whatever **he says or does**.

οὐ παύσομαι ζητοῦσα πρὶν αὐτὸ **εὕρω** ἄν. = I will not stop searching until
I find it [whenever that might be].

§ 153 Subjunctive after ἵνα, ὅπως, ὡς, or μή in a purpose clause or in an effort clause when purpose implied

- negative μή

οἱ Λακεδαιμόνιοι ἔρχονται ἵνα τὴν πόλιν **λάβωνται**. = The Spartans are coming in order that **they may take** the city. *or* The Spartans are coming **to take** the city.

εἶμι Ἀθηνάζε ὅπως ὑπὸ Σωκράτους **διδαχθῶ**. = I will go to Athens in order that **I may be taught** by Socrates. *or* I will go to Athens **to be taught** by Socrates.

οἱ πρυτάνεις τοὺς πολίτας καλοῦσιν ἐπὶ τὴν ἐκκλησίαν ὡς περὶ τῆς εἰρήνης οἱ Λακεδαιμόνιοι αὐτοῖς **λέγωσιν**. = The prytaneis are summoning the citizens to the assembly in order that the Spartans **may speak** to them about peace.

§ 154 Subjunctive after μή in a fear clause for future

δείδω μὴ ἡ πόλις **ληφθῇ** ὑπὸ τῶν ἐχθρῶν. = I am afraid that the city **may be taken** [*or* **will be taken**] by the enemy.

- A fear clause indicating a fear that something may not happen uses μή + οὐ.

φοβοῦμαι **μὴ οὐχ** ἡ πόλις **σωθῇ**. = I fear that the city **may not be saved** [*or* **will not be saved**].

Optative mood (§§155–159)

Optative mood: two common independent uses (§§155–156)

§ 155 Optative of wish for future

- by itself or accompanied by εἴθε or εἰ γάρ

σώσειεν ὁ θεὸς τὴν πόλιν. = **May** the god **save** the city.
εἴθε φυλάττοιεν οἱ θεοὶ τὴν πόλιν. = **May** the gods **protect** the city.

§ 156 Potential optative (§161)

- accompanied by ἄν
- translate: "might, could, would, should ——"

σώσειεν ἄν ὁ θεὸς τὴν πόλιν. = The god **might/could save** the city.
σώσειας ἄν τὴν ἡμετέραν πόλιν; = **Would you save** our city?

Optative mood: three common dependent uses (i.e., always in dependent clauses) (§§157–159)

§ 157 Optative in future-less-vivid condition (also called future remote, hypothetical, or should-would condition) (§161, §164)

- Sentence contains two optatives, one in a conditional ("if") clause, one in the main clause with ἄν.
- translate: "if *x* were to/should ——, *y* would —— . . ."

> εἰ οἱ πολῖται τῇ θεᾷ **θύοιεν, σώσειεν ἄν** τὴν πόλιν. = If the citizens **were to sacrifice** to the goddess, she **would/might save** the city. *or* If the citizens **should sacrifice** to the goddess, she **would save** the city.

§ 158 Optative in indirect statements or questions

- Optative in indirect statements (after ὅτι/ὡς) or indirect questions is commonly used to represent an indicative after a main verb in secondary (past) tense.[7]
- The tense of the optative represents the tense of the indicative in the original direct statement or question.

> present optative: Σωκράτης εἶπεν ὅτι οὐκ **εἰδείη** οὐδέν. = Socrates said that he **did** not **know** anything. [original statement: I don't know anything.]
> future optative: ἠρόμην ὅπου **δυνησοίμην** ἰδεῖν ταῦτα. = I asked where I **would be able** to see these things. [original question: Where will I be able to see these things?]
> aorist optative: οἱ ἄγγελλοι εἶπον ὅτι οἱ πολέμιοι τὴν πόλιν **λάβοι.** = The messengers said that the enemy **had taken** the city. *or less formally* The messengers said that the enemy **took** the city. [original statement: The enemy took the city.]
> perfect optative: ὁ ξένος ἤρετο ὅστις τούτους τοὺς νόμους **τέθηκοι.** = The stranger asked who **had established** those laws. [original question: Who has established these laws?]

§ 159 Optative replacing subjunctive in dependent clauses after a main verb in secondary[8] (past) tense (cf. §§152–154)

a. past general (cf. present general with subjunctive; §152)
- in conditional, conditional relative, or temporal clauses
- signals a generalization or indefinite time frame in past time
- translate: "if [ever], whenever, whoever, until" + past indicative
- no ἄν!

---

7. Secondary tenses are augmented: imperfect, aorist, pluperfect.
8. Secondary tenses are augmented: imperfect, aorist, pluperfect.

εἰ Σωκράτης **εἴποι**, ἐθαύμαζον αὐτοῦ ἀκούσας. = If [**ever**] Socrates **spoke**, I was amazed upon hearing him. [past general condition; distinguish from future-less-vivid]

ἐθαύμαζον ὅτε **ἴδοιμι** τὴν πόλιν. = I was amazed when**ever I saw** the city.

ᾔεις ὅποι **βούλοιο**. = You went wher**ever you wished**.

ἔγωγε ἐπιμελὲς ἐποίουν ἑκάστης ἡμέρας εἰδέναι ὅ τι Σωκράτης **λέγοι ἢ πράττοι**. = I for my part used to make it my practice each day to know what**ever** Socrates **said or did**.

οὐκ ἐπαυόμην ζητοῦσα πρὶν αὐτὸ **εὕροιμι**. = I did not stop searching until **I found** it.

b. optative to replace subjunctive in purpose clauses (after ἵνα, ὅπως, ὡς, μή) in secondary sequence (main verb in past tense; §153)

οἱ Λακεδαιμόνιοι ἦλθον ἵνα τὴν πόλιν **λάβοιντο**. = The Spartans came in order that **they might take** the city. or The Spartans came **to take** the city.

c. optative to replace subjunctive in fear clauses (after verb of fearing + μή) in secondary sequence (main verb in past tense; §154)

ἐδείσαμεν μὴ ἡ πόλις **ληφθείη** ὑπὸ τῶν ἐχθρῶν. = We were afraid that the city **might be taken** [or **would be taken**] by the enemy.

- A fear clause indicating a fear that something may not happen uses μή + οὐ.

ἐφοβούμην μὴ **οὐχ** ἡ πόλις **σωθείη**. = I feared that the city **might not be saved** [or **would not be saved**].

Common uses of ἄν (§§160–162)

§ 160 Ἄν + subjunctive (§152)

- *Basic significance*: to generalize or express indefinite time frame to action in primary sequence; the sense is best expressed in English by present indicative; the word *ever* may be added to signal the indefinite or general quality of the action.
- *Context*: occurs within conditional, relative, and temporal clauses (note: ἄν + εἰ = ἐάν, ἤν, or ἄν; ἄν + ὅτε = ὅταν; ἄν + ἐπειδή = ἐπειδάν).

conditional: **ἐὰν** τὴν ἀλήθειαν **εὕρωμεν**, εὐδαίμονες ἐσόμεθα. = **If ever we discover** the truth, we will be happy.

relative: γάμει ὃν **ἂν ἐθέλῃς**. = Marry whom**ever you wish**.

temporal: **ὅταν εἴπωμεν**, πάντες θαυμάζουσιν. = When**ever we speak**, all are amazed.

αὐτοῦ μενοῦμεν ἕως **ἂν** ὁ ἀδελφὸς **ἀφίκηται**. = We will wait here until our brother **arrives** [whenever that might be].

- Types of condition

  ≈ Present general: offers a generalization in present time.

  ἐὰν οἱ νέοι τοὺς θεοὺς τιμῶσιν, ἀεὶ πολὺ ἐπαινῶ. = If ever the young honor the gods, I always praise [them] greatly.
  ὅταν εἴπῃς, ἀκούουσιν οἱ νέοι. = Whenever you speak, the young men listen.
  ὅποι ἂν ἴω, λέγοντος ἐμοῦ ἀκούουσιν οἱ νέοι. = Wherever I go, the young men listen to me speaking.

  ≈ Future-more-vivid: so-called to distinguish it from the more hypothetical future condition with the optative (future-less-vivid); this categorization, however, obscures that future-more-vivid conditions are very frequently generalizations set in future time and might just as well be called future general.

  ἐὰν ᾖς φιλομαθής, ἔσει πολυμαθής. = If you are a lover of learning, you will be very learned. [Isocrates]
  ὅποι ἂν ἴω, λέγοντος ἐμοῦ ἀκούσονται οἱ νέοι. = Wherever I go, the young men will listen to me speaking.

  ≈ Other: the main clause (apodosis) sometimes contains neither a present indicative nor a future indicative, but is replaced by other moods referring to present or future time (e.g., imperative, hortatory, or prohibitive subjunctive).

  ἐὰν τὴν ἀλήθειαν μάθῃς, εἰπέ με. = If ever you learn the truth, tell me.
  ὡς ἂν ἐγὼ εἴπω, πειθώμεθα. = However I speak, let us obey.
  ἕπου ὅπη ἂν ἐκεῖνος ἡγῆται. = Follow wherever that man leads.
  ὅ τι ἐκεῖνος ἂν λέγῃ, μὴ ἀκούσατε. = Whatever he says, don't listen.

§ 161 Ἄν + optative
- = potential optative (§156) or in apodosis of future-less-vivid condition (§157)
- *Basic significance*: to express a potential or hypothetical situation (future time); the sense is best captured by English modals: "might/could/would/should/may."
- *Context*: main or dependent clause.

  ≈ Unlike ἄν + subjunctive (§160), ἄν + optative is typically found in the main clause.

  ἡ ἐμὴ σοφία φαύλη τις **ἂν εἴη**. = My wisdom **might be** something worthless.
  ἴσως **ἂν** ἐγὼ **λέγοιμι** ἀληθῶς περὶ τοῦ μεθύσκεσθαι. = Perhaps **I may speak** truthfully about getting drunk.
  τί **εἴποις ἄν**, Σώκρατες; = What **would you say**, Socrates?

≈ But it can be in a dependent clause with no change of meaning or function.

θαυμάζω καὶ αὐτὸς ποῦ **ἂν εἴη**. = I myself also wonder where **he could be**.
σκοπεῖσθε οὖν τίνι τρόπῳ **ἂν** ὡς ῥᾷστα **πίνοιμεν**. = So consider in what way **we might drink** as easily [unproblematically] as possible.

- *Type of condition*: future-less-vivid (also called future improbable, future remote, should-would): though ἄν + optative is very likely to occur independently (potential optative), it may also be accompanied by a conditional clause containing another optative (without ἄν); both contexts express a hypothetical or potential situation (note the translation of the optative in the "if" clause).

  εἰ **μεθύσκοισθε, καταγελῷμεν** ἄν. = If **you should become drunk, we would laugh** [at you]. *or* If **you were to become drunk, we would laugh** [at you].
  φαίη δ᾽ **ἂν** ἡ θανοῦσα γ᾽ εἰ φωνὴν **λάβοι**. = The dead woman, for her part, **would speak**, if **she could obtain** a voice. [Sophocles, *Electra*]

§ 162 Ἄν + indicative

- *Basic significance*: to express an idea that is contrary-to-fact (counterfactual, unreal).

  ≈ imperfect indicative: contrary-to-fact (present): "would be ——ing, would ——"

  ≈ aorist indicative: contrary-to-fact (past): "would have ——ed"

- *Context*: main clause; unlike ἄν + subjunctive (§160), but like ἄν + optative (§161), ἄν + indicative is not found within dependent clauses, but is typically found in the main clause of a sentence and particularly in the apodosis of a conditional sentence; even when it occurs without an if-clause, some conditional idea is usually implied.

  οὐ γὰρ **ἂν προαπέστης**. = For **you would** not **have come away first**. [implied: if you had not discovered something]

- *Type of condition*: contrary-to-fact (present, past, or mixed) (unreal, unfulfilled).

  ≈ present contrary-to-fact

  εἰ ἀγαθὸς **ἦν** ἐκεῖνος, ἐγὼ **ἐτίμων ἄν**, νῦν δὲ οὐκ ἔστιν ἀγαθός. = If that man **were** good, **I would honor** him, but now he is not good.
  εἰ οἱ ῥήτορες βελτίους **ἦσαν**, οὕτως ἀσθενὴς **οὐκ ἦν ἂν** αὕτη ἡ πόλις. = If the politicians **were** better, this city **would not be** so weak.

εἰ μὴ ὁ φαῦλος τοσοῦτον οἶνον **ἔπινεν**, οὕτως αἰσχρῶς **οὐκ ἐμεθύσκετο ἄν.** = If the worthless man **did not [habitually] drink** so much wine, **he would not get** so disgracefully **drunk**.

≈ past contrary-to-fact

εἰ **ἠκούσαμεν** τῆς μαντικῆς, ἡ πόλις **ἐσώθη ἄν.** = If **we had listened** to the prophetic woman, the city **would have been saved**.

εἰ πάλαι ταῦτα ἡμῖν **εἶπες**, οὐκ **ἠκούσαμεν ἄν.** = If **you had told** us these things long ago, **we would** not **have listened**.

≈ mixed tenses

εἰ μὴ ὑμεῖς **ἤλθετε, ἐπορευόμεθα** ἄν ἐπὶ βασιλέα. = If **you had** not **come, we would be marching** against the king.

εἰ ὑμεῖς σοφώτεροι **ἦτε**, τοιαῦτα οὐκ **ἐποιήσατε** ἄν. = If you **were** wiser, **you would** not **have done** such things.

Conditional sentences (§§163–165; see also §§160–162)

§ 163 Conditions without ἄν

- Simple conditions: most conditions without ἄν are simple conditions that use the indicative; generally, it is safe to translate the verbs as in other contexts.
- Past general conditions (§159a): the only other type of condition without ἄν is the past general condition; this is signaled by an optative in a conditional, relative, or temporal clause; the main clause contains a past tense, usually an imperfect indicative.

§ 164 Summary of important conditions

condition	if-clause (protasis)	main clause (apodosis)
present contrary-to-fact (present unreal, unfulfilled)	εἰ + imperfect indicative: "if x were ——ing"	imperfect indicative + ἄν: "y would be ——ing"
past contrary-to-fact (past unreal, unfulfilled)	εἰ + aorist indicative: "if x had ——ed"	aorist indicative + ἄν: "y would have ——ed"
future-less-vivid (future remote, improbable, should-would)	εἰ + optative: "if x should —— or if x were to ——"	optative + ἄν: "y would ——"
present general	ἐάν + subjunctive: "if [ever] x ——s"	present indicative: "y ——s"
past general	εἰ + optative: "if x [ever] ——ed"	past indicative: "y ——ed"
future-more-vivid	ἐάν + subjunctive: "if [ever] x ——s"	future indicative: "y will ——"

§ 165 Examples of important conditions

- present contrary-to-fact

  εἰ οἱ θεοὶ τῶν ἀνθρώπων ἐπεμελοῦντο, οὕτως οὐκ ἐπάσχομεν ἄν. = If the gods cared for men, we would not be suffering in this way.

- past contrary-to-fact

  εἰ ὁ προφήτης σαφέστερον εἶπεν, ἡ πόλις ἂν ἐσώθη. = If the prophet had spoken more clearly, the city would have been saved.

- future-less-vivid

  εἰ εἴποις, ἡ πόλις ἂν σωθείη. = If you were to speak, the city would be saved.

- present general

  ἆρα βελτίονες γιγνόμεθα, ἐὰν πολλὰ μάθωμεν; = Do we become better, if we learn many things?

- past general

  ἆρα οἱ νεανίαι βελτίονες ἐγένοντο, εἰ τῶν φιλοσοφῶν ἀκούοιεν; = Did the young men become better, if they listened to philosophers?

- future-more-vivid

  ἐὰν οἱ πολῖται τοῖς νόμοις πείθηται, ἡ πόλις βελτίων γενήσεται. = If the citizens obey the laws, the city will become better.

Verbs: Nonfinite (Participle and Infinitive)

Participles (§§166–178)

§ 166 Participle: definition and general principles

- A participle is a verbal adjective.
- A participle agrees in case, number, and gender with a noun or pronoun in the sentence expressed or understood.
- A participle is not a finite verb; it does not have person and cannot be the main verb of the sentence.
- basic translations

	active/middle		passive
present	——ing		being ——ed
future	about to ——, in order to ——		about to be ——ed, in order to be ——ed
aorist	upon ——ing, having ——ed		upon being ——ed, having been ——ed
perfect	having ——ed		having been ——ed

- present active

  οἱ ἄνδρες ἐπέρχονται **τρέχοντες**. = The men attack **running**. *or* **Running,** the men attack.

- aorist active

  ἰδὼν τὴν πόλιν, ὁ στρατηγὸς αὐτοὺς ἐκέλευσεν ἐπελθεῖν. = **Upon seeing** the city, the general ordered them to attack.

- In English, the participle usually agrees with the subject; this is not true in Greek, which means that sometimes the participle must be translated by a clause with finite verbs for acceptable English.

  τὸ δ᾽ ἄστυ **καλὸν ὂν** οὐ τιμῶ. = I do not honor the city, **[it] being beautiful**. [unacceptable English] *or* I do not honor the city, **although it is beautiful**. [acceptable English]

§ 167 Tense/aspect of participle

- Participle tense is only relative to the tense of the main verb; sometimes aspect rather than tense is relevant when dealing with a participle.
  - ≈ Present participle describes action *ongoing at the time of* the main verb.
  - ≈ Future participle describes action *in the future relative to* the main verb.
  - ≈ Aorist participle describes either action *preceding* the main verb (tense) or a simple action *accompanying* the main verb (rather than ongoing action) (aspect).
  - ≈ Perfect participle describes action *complete at the time of* the main verb.

- present participle

  νέος ὤν, δύναμαι πολλὰ μανθάνειν. = **Being** young, I am able to learn many things. *or* **Since I am** young, I am able to learn many things.

  νέος ὤν, ἐδυνάμην πολλὰ μανθάνειν. = **Being** young, I was able to learn many things. *or* **When I was** young, I was able to learn many things. *or* **Since I was** young, I was able to learn many things.

- future participle

  ὁ γέρων οἶδε τὰ **ἐσόμενα**. = The old man knows the things **that will be**. [substantive participle; see §169]

  ὁ γέρων ἦλθεν **λυσόμενος** τὴν θυγάτερα. = The old man went **to ransom** his daughter. [future participle often shows purpose; §172]

- aorist participle

  βλέψας εἰς ἐμέ, ἐγέλασεν. = **Upon looking** at me, he laughed. *or* **Having looked** at me, he laughed. [emphasizes aorist tense] *or* **With a glance** at me, he laughed. [emphasizes aspect] *or* He **looked** at me and laughed. [simple action accompanying the main verb]

- perfect participle

  ἄλλος γάρ τις μοι διηγεῖτο **ἀκηκοὼς** Φοίνικος τοῦ Φιλίππου. = For someone else, **having heard** [it] from Phoinix the son of Philippos, told me.

Four basic uses of the participle (§§168–171)

§ 168 Attributive use of the participle

- participle in attributive position, i.e., following the definite article (not necessarily immediately) (§122)
- acts as an adjective
- often best translated by a relative clause

ὁ **καθεύδων** κύων = the **sleeping** dog

ὁ **δραμὼν** εἰς τὴν ἀγορὰν κύων = the dog **that ran** into the agora

οἱ ἄλλοι οἱ τότε ἐν τῷ δείπνῳ **παραγενόμενοι** = the others **who were present** at the dinner at that time

§ 169 Substantive use of the participle

- participle accompanied by definite article
- similar to attributive, but no other noun or substantive expressed
- missing noun inferred from gender and number of definite article and participle
- acts as a noun

ὁ **καθεύδων** = **the sleeping man**

τὰ ἄρτι γεγενημένα = **the things that have happened** recently

αἱ πεμφθεῖαι εἰς τὴν πόλιν = **the women who were sent** to the city

οἱ τότε ἐν τῷ δείπνῳ **παραγενόμενοι** = **those who were present** at the dinner at that time

§ 170 Supplementary use of the participle

- with certain verbs and in certain expressions (e.g., τυγχάνω, λανθάνω, παύομαι, ἄρχομαι, χαίρω, ἥδομαι, δῆλός ἐστι, φαίνομαι, φθάνω, and verbs with similar meanings)
- participle in predicate position (not following definite article; §123)
- take closely with the verb, often with special translation (note especially τυγχάνω, λανθάνω, δῆλός ἐστι, φαίνομαι)

- ἐτύγχανον χθὲς εἰς ἄστυ **ἰών.** = Yesterday I happened to be going to the city.

ὁ ἀγαθὸς χαίρει τοῖς νόμοις **πειθόμενος.** = The good man enjoys **obeying** the laws.

ὁ κακὸς οὔποτε παύεται ἄλλους **βλάπτων.** = The bad man never stops **harming** others.

ἔλαθον τοὺς φύλακας **φυγόντες.** = They escaped the notice of the guards **in fleeing.** or **In fleeing**, they escaped the notice of the guards. [i.e., the guards didn't notice them fleeing]

ἐτύγχανε **θύσας.** = He happened **to have sacrificed.**

ἐτύγχανε **θύων.** = He happened **to be sacrificing.**

δῆλός ἐστι **ἀδικῶν.** = He is clearly **being unjust.**

φαίνεται μῶρος **ὤν.** = He shows **he is** foolish. or He reveals **himself to be** foolish. (Compare translation of φαίνομαι + inf., §180)

τρία ἔτη ἐστίν ἀφ' οὗ ἐγὼ Σωκράτει **συνδιατρίβων** ἠρξάμην. = It is three years since I began **spending time** with Socrates.

§ 171 Circumstantial use of the participle

- most common use
- participle in predicate position (not following definite article; §123)
- describes circumstances under which the action of the main verb takes place (adverbial)
- range of ways to translate, including finite clauses beginning with "when, since, although, if"

> τῶν οὖν γνωρίμων τις ὄπισθεν **ἰδών** με πόρρωθεν ἐκάλεσε, καὶ **παίζων** εἶπεν. = So one of my acquaintances, **upon seeing** me from behind from a distance called [me], and he spoke, **joking**.
>
> **ἀφικόμενος** ἐπὶ τῷ δείπνῳ, τι γελοῖον ἔπαθον. = **Upon arriving** at the dinner party, I experienced something ridiculous.
>
> **δραμὼν** εἰς τὴν ἀγοράν, ὁ κῆρυξ ἤγγειλε τὴν νίκην. = **Having run** into the agora, the herald announced the victory. or The herald **ran** into the agora **and** announced the victory.
>
> ἑταῖρος Σωκράτους **ὤν**, δικαιότατος εἶ τοὺς λόγους αὐτοῦ ἀπαγγέλλειν. = **Being** Socrates' companion, you are the best one to publicize his words. or **Since you are** Socrates' companion, you are the best one to publicize his words.

Special uses of the circumstantial and supplementary participle (§§172–178)

§ 172 Future participle (circumstantial), with or without ὡς, indicates purpose

> οἱ Λακεδαιμόνιοι ἦλθον Ἀθήναζε [**ὡς**] τὸ ἄστυ **αἱρήσοντες**. = The Spartans came to Athens **with the intention of taking** the city. or The Spartans came to Athens **in order to take** the city.

§ 173 Μή + participle (circumstantial) usually has conditional ("if") force

> **μὴ** χρήματα **δούς**, οὐκ ἂν ἐλύθην. = **If not having given** money, I would not have been released. or **If I hadn't given** money, I would not have been released.

- Context may also suggest conditional force when not accompanied by negative.

> ταῦτα **εἰδὼς** ὑμῖν ἂν εἶπον. = **If I knew** those things, I would have told you.

§ 174 Ἄτε + participle (circumstantial) has causal ("because, since") force

> **ἄτε** οὐχ οἷός τ' **ὤν** τὴν γυναῖκα λιπεῖν, ἔμεινεν ἐν τῇ πόλει. = **Because of** not **being** able to leave his wife, he remained in the city. or **Because he was** not able to leave his wife, he remained in the city.

§ **175** Καίπερ + participle (circumstantial) has concessive ("although") force

καίπερ ἄριστος τῶν Ἑλλήνων **ὤν**, Αἴας ἱκανῶς οὐκ ἐτιμᾶτο. = **Although being** the best of the Greeks, Ajax was not honored sufficiently. or **Although he was** the best of the Greeks, Ajax was not honored sufficiently.

§ **176** Participle (circumstantial) in a genitive absolute
- genitive participle agreeing with noun or pronoun in genitive, not part of main clause
- genitive noun or pronoun acting as subject of genitive absolute
- best translated as a finite clause introduced by "when, since, although, while, if"
- The tense of the participle is relative to that of the main verb, so that, for example, a present participle describes an ongoing action in the past if the main verb is a past tense.

πάλαι ἐγένετο ἡ συνουσία αὕτη, **παίδων ὄντων ἡμῶν ἔτι.** = This gathering happened long ago, **with us still being children.** or This gathering happened long ago, **when we were still children.**

μένοντος ἐμοῦ ὁ Σωκράτης ἐκέλευσε προϊέναι ἄνευ αὐτοῦ. = **With me waiting**, Socrates urged [me] to go ahead without him. or **Although I was waiting**, Socrates urged [me] to go ahead without him. or **While I was waiting**, Socrates urged [me] to go ahead without him.

μετὰ ταῦτα, **κατακλινέντος τοῦ Σωκράτους καὶ δειπνήσαντος**, σπονδὰς ἐποιησάμεθα. = After these things, **with Socrates having reclined and dined**, we made libations. or After this, **when Socrates had reclined and dined**, we made libations.

§ **177** Participle (circumstantial) in an accusative absolute
- similar to genitive absolute but used with impersonal constructions only
- uses neuter singular accusative participle typically of impersonal verb (e.g., δέον from δεῖ; ἐξόν from ἔξεστι) [+ accusative or dative] + infinitive
- best translated as a finite clause introduced by "when, since, although, while, if"

οὐκ ἐξὸν εἰρήνην ἄγειν, εὖ μαχώμεθα. = **It not being possible to live in peace**, let us fight well. or **Since it is not possible to live in peace**, let us fight well.

φύλακά με τοῦ λόγου ἀναγκάζεις γίγνεσθαι τοῦ σεαυτοῦ, **ἐξόν σοι ἐν εἰρήνῃ λέγειν.** = You force me to become a guardian of your speech, **it being possible for you to speak in peace.** or You force me to become a guardian of your speech, **when it is possible for you to speak in peace.** or You force me to become a guardian of your speech, **although it is possible for you to speak in peace.**

νῦν τούτων οὐδὲν γίγνεται, **δέον πάντα γίγνεσθαι.** = None of these things is now happening, **it being necessary for all of them to happen.** *or* None of these things is now happening, **although they all ought to be happening.**

§ 178 Participle (supplementary) serving as the verb in indirect discourse

- This form of indirect statement typically follows a verb of knowing (e.g., οἶδα, γιγνώσκω, ἐπίσταμαι), showing (e.g., δηλόω, δείκνυμι, φαίνω, ἀγγέλλω), perceiving (e.g., αἰσθάνομαι, πυνθάνομαι, ἀκούω, ὁράω, βλέπω), or learning (e.g., εὑρίσκω, μανθάνω).
- If the subject of the indirect statement is *different* from the subject of the main verb, it is put in the *accusative* case; the participle matches the case, number, and gender of the accusative.

ἐπυθόμην **ὑμᾶς φαγόντας** πάντα. = I learned **that you ate** everything. *or* I learned **that you had eaten** everything. [aorist participle active]

ἀκούω **αὐτοὺς** χεῖρας **βεβλαμμένους.** = I hear **that they have been harmed** with respect to their hands. [perfect participle passive]

οἶδα **αὐτοὺς** οὔποτε τοῦτο **ποιήσοντας.** = I know **that they will** never **do** this. [future active participle]

- If the subject of the indirect statement is *the same as* the subject of the main verb, no new subject is expressed; the participle is nominative agreeing in case, number, and gender with the subject.

οἶδα σοφὸς οὐκ **ὤν.** = I know [that] **I am** not wise.

Uses of the infinitive (§§179–185)

§ 179 Complementary infinitive

- with verbs and expressions that denote wishing or wanting (e.g., βούλομαι, ἐθέλω); hoping, expecting, or intending (e.g., μέλλω, ἐλπίζω); seeming (e.g., δοκέω, ἔοικα); capability (e.g., ἔχω, οἷός τ᾽ εἰμί, δύναμαι, ἐπίσταμαι); attempting (e.g., πειράομαι); or daring (e.g., τολμάω)

βούλομαι **πυθέσθαι.** = I wish **to learn.**

ἐκεῖνος οὐκ εἶχεν οὐδὲν σαφὲς **λέγειν.** = He was not able **to say** anything clear.

πάντα πειράσομαι σαφῶς **διηγεῖσθαι.** = I will try **to describe** everything clearly.

ἐκεῖνος φαίνεται μῶρος **εἶναι.** = He appears **to be** foolish. *or* He seems **to be** foolish. (Compare translation of φαίνομαι + part., §170)

§ 180 Objective infinitive

- with accusative after verbs of commanding, willing, wishing, making (e.g., κελεύω, ἐθέλω, βούλομαι, ἀναγκάζω)

κελεύω σε **λέγειν**. = I order you **to speak**.
βούλομαι σε **λέγειν**. = I want you **to speak**.
οἱ λόγοι ἐκείνου ποιοῦσιν αὐτοὺς **κατέχεσθαι**. = His words causes them **to be bewitched**.

§ 181 Explanatory or epexegetical infinitive

- with adjectives that denote fitness or capacity (ἀγαθός, δεινός, δίκαιος, δυνατός, ἐπιτηδεῖος, σοφός) or the lack of it (ἀδύνατος)

οὔκ εἰμι δεινὸς **λέγειν**. = I am not clever **at speaking**.
Σωκράτης τε καὶ Ἀριστοφάνης δυνατώτατοι **πίνειν**. = Socrates and Aristophanes are most capable **at drinking**.
ἑταῖρος Σωκράτους ὤν, εἶ δικαιότατος τοὺς λόγους αὐτοῦ **ἀγγέλλειν**. = Being Socrates' companion, you are most suitable **for announcing** his words.

§ 182 Infinitive acting as a noun in a sentence

- equivalent of English gerund
- usually with neuter singular definite article (articular infinitive)

χαλεπὸν **τὸ εὖ λέγειν**. = **Speaking well** is difficult. [nominative articular infinitive acting as subject of sentence]
τῷ εὖ λέγειν ἐπείθομεν τοὺς ἀκούοντας. = **By speaking well** we persuaded those listening. [dative articular infinitive: dative of means]
διὰ **τὸ Σωκράτη ἀληθῆ λέγειν** οἱ πολῖται ἐδεδίησαν. = **Because of Socrates' speaking the truth**, the citizens were afraid. [accusative articular infinitive: object of the preposition διά; here the articular infinitive also has an accusative subject: Socrates]
περιφερῆ ἦν αὐτὰ διὰ **τὸ τοῖς γονεῦσιν ὅμοια εἶναι**. = They themselves were round, because of **being like their parents**. [accusative articular infinitive: object of the preposition διά; here the subject of the articular infinitive is the same as the subject of the main verb so is not expressed]
θαυμάζω **τὸ εὖ λέγειν**. = I admire **good speaking**. [accusative articular infinitive serving as direct object]
τοῦ εὖ λέγειν ἕνεκα ποιήσω ταῦτα. = For the sake of **speaking well**, I will do these things. [genitive articular infinitive: object of the preposition ἕνεκα]

- Sometimes an infinitive being used this way will not have the definite article. As often, the definite article is omitted on a predicate (see §188), as in the next two examples.

  (1) τὸ ὀρθὰ δοξάζειν καὶ ἄνευ (2) τοῦ ἔχειν λόγον δοῦναι οὔτε (3) ἐπίστασθαί ἐστιν οὔτε ἀμαθία. = (1) **Holding an opinion correctly** even without (2) **being able to offer a reasoned explanation** is neither (3) **knowing** nor ignorance. [(1) nominative articular infinitive = subject; (2) genitive articular infinitive = object of the preposition ἄνευ; (3) nominative infinitive = predicate]

  τὸ θύειν δωρεῖσθαί ἐστι τοῖς θεοῖς. = **Sacrificing** is **giving gifts** to the gods. [nominative articular infinitive = subject; nominative infinitive = predicate]

§ 183 Infinitive in impersonal constructions

- with δεῖ, χρή, ἔξεστι, δοκεῖ, ἀνάγκη/ἀναγκαῖον ἐστί

  δεῖ με πιεῖν τοῦτον τὸν οἶνον. = It is necessary for me **to drink** this wine.

§ 184 Infinitive serving as the verb in indirect statement

- after a verb of asserting or believing (e.g., φημί, νομίζω, δοκέω, ἡγέομαι, οἴομαι/οἶμαι)
- The tense of the infinitive preserves the tense of the original statement.

  οὗτος δέ φησι καὶ σὲ τὸν λόγον **εἰδέναι**. = And he says that you also **know** the story. [present infinitive]

  ὁ δ᾽ Ἀπολλόδωρος οὔ φησι τῇ συνουσίᾳ **παραγένεσθαι**. = Apollodorus says that he **was** not **present** at the gathering. [aorist infinitive] [οὔ φημι = I deny that, I say that . . . not; ≠ I don't say]

  οὗτος δέ φησι τῇ ὑστεραίᾳ τῷ δείπνῳ **παραγενήσεσθαι**. = He says that he **will be present** at the dinner on the following day. [future infinitive]

  ἆρ᾽ ἡγῇ ταύτην τὴν συνουσίαν νεωστὶ **γεγονέναι**; = Do you think that this gathering **happened** recently? [perfect infinitive]

- A present infinitive normally represents an original imperfect indicative (since there is no imperfect infinitive); context determines that the speaker is describing the past.

  οἶμαι τοῦτον τὸν ἄνδρα σωφρονέστατον τῶν τότ᾽ **εἶναι**. = I think this man **was** the most moderate of people at that time. [τότε here signals that the speaker is talking about the past]

- After main verbs in the past, the translation of the verb in indirect statement needs to be adjusted to reflect English practice (which normally shifts the tense).

ἔφη δὲ καὶ σὲ **εἰδέναι**. = And he said you also **knew**. [present infinitive]

ἔφασαν δὲ τῇ ὑστεραίᾳ τῷ δείπνῳ **παραγενήσεσθαι**. = They said that they **would be present** at the dinner the next day. [future infinitive representing an original statement in the future after main verb in past tense]

- If the subject of the indirect statement is *different* from the subject of the main verb, it is put in the *accusative* case.

οὔ φαμεν **αὐτοὺς δραμεῖσθαι** θᾶττον τῶν ἵππων. = We deny **that they will run** more swiftly than the horses. [future infinitive] [οὔ φημι = I deny that, I say that . . . not; ≠ I don't say]

ἔφαμεν **αὐτοὺς** ἱκανὸν οἶνον ἤδη **πεπωκέναι**. = We said **that they had** already **drunk** enough wine. [perfect infinitive after verb in past tense]

- If the subject of the indirect statement is *the same as* the subject of the main verb, no new subject is expressed.

νομίζω **εἰδέναι** ὀλίγα. = I think **that I know** a few things.

Σωκράτης οὐκ ἔφη οὐδὲν **εἰδέναι**. = Socrates denied **that he knew** anything. [οὔ φημι = I deny that, I say that . . . not; ≠ I don't say]

οὐχ ὁμολογήσω ἄκλητος **ἥκειν**. = I will not admit **that I have come** uninvited.

§ 185 Infinitive serving as the verb in a natural result clause (after ὥστε) or a πρίν-clause

- Natural result clause: ὥστε [+ accusative] + infinitive describes the possible or expected consequence of the circumstances described in the main clause; it does not tell whether that result actually is happening, has happened, or will happen.
- Ὥστε + indicative emphasizes that the result actually took place (actual result clause).
- Latinists should distinguish from Latin usage, which consistently uses subjunctive for result clauses.

ἆρ' ἡγῇ ταύτην τὴν συνουσίαν νεωστὶ γεγονέναι ὥστε καὶ ἐμὲ **παραγενέσθαι**; = Do you think this gathering happened so recently that I too **was present**? [*implying*: so recently that I too could have been present]

θέλω ὑμᾶς συμφησῆσαι ὥστε δύ' ὄντας ἕνα **γεγονέναι**. = I am willing to fuse you together so that although you are two **you become** one.

≈ An actual result clause does not use the infinitive but the indicative.

Ἄλκεστις ἔργον οὕτω καλὸν ἠργάσατο, ὥστε αὐτὴν καὶ οἱ θεοί **ἐτίμησαν**. = Alcestis accomplished a deed so great that even the gods **honored** her. [indicative makes clear that this was the actual result]

- πρίν + [accusative] + infinitive

πρὶν **μαθεῖν** ταῦτα καθεύδωμεν. = Before **learning** these things, let us sleep. *or* Before **we learn** these things, let us sleep.

ὁ κῆρυξ τὴν νικὴν ἤγγειλε πρὶν τοὺς στρατηγοὺς **ἀφικέσθαι**. = The herald announced the victory before the generals **arrived**. [the accusative τοὺς στρατηγούς is the subject of the πρίν-clause]

Definite Article

§ 186 Definite article with a noun or an adjective + noun

- translate: "the"

  ὁ ἄνθρωπος = the man
  τὴν καλὴν νῆσον = the beautiful island

- Greek sometimes uses a definite article with a noun where English does not. It is not translated in these contexts.

  ≈ before proper nouns

  ὁ Σωκράτης = Socrates

  ≈ accompanying possessive adjectives

  τὸν ὑμέτερον λόγον = your word
  ἡ ἐμὴ γυνή = my wife

  ≈ accompanying demonstrative adjectives

  τὸν παῖδα τοῦτον = this child/slave
  ἐκεῖνο τὸ πάθος = that suffering [note correct position of demonstrative + definite article]

  ≈ accompanying abstract nouns

  ἡ ἀρετή = virtue, excellence
  ἡ σοφία = wisdom

§ 187 Definite article to create attributive phrases

- It is common to insert a phrase (e.g., in the genitive) between the definite article and the noun agreeing with it in case, number, and gender, when that phrase describes the noun.

  οἱ ἱκέται τῶν τοῦ βασιλέως ποδῶν ἐλάβοντο. = The suppliants took hold of the king's feet. [the position of τοῦ βασιλέως between τῶν and ποδῶν shows that it describes ποδῶν] οἱ πολῖται τὰς ἐν τῇ πόλει γυναῖκας ἐτίμων. = The citizens honored the women in the city. [the position of ἐν τῇ πόλει between τὰς and γυναῖκας shows that it describes γυναῖκας]

- The definite article may be repeated following the noun to indicate that the adjective or a phrase describes a noun in the same case, number, and gender; sometimes this suggests an afterthought.

ἡ ὁδὸς ἡ εἰς ἄστυ = the road into the city
ὁ πολίτης ὁ ἀγαθὸς τὴν ἀλήθειαν ἀεὶ λέγει. = The good citizen always speaks the truth. or The citizen—that is, the good one—always speaks the truth. [the repetition of ὁ shows that ἀγαθὸς describes πολίτης]
μεγάλη ἡ σοφία **ἡ Σωκράτους**. = The wisdom **of Socrates** is great. or **Socrates'** wisdom is great.

§ 188 Definite article omitted on predicate
- The definite article is *usually* omitted on predicate nouns; its absence can therefore help identify a noun as predicate (§73, §78).

μετὰ ὀλίγον χρόνον **ἄριστοι πολῖται** οἱ ξένοι ἐγένοντο. = After a short time, the foreigners became **the best citizens**.
ἆρ᾽ οἱ Ἕλληνες πολλάκις **στρατηγοὺς** ἐποιήσαντο τοὺς μεγίστους ποιητάς; = Did the Greeks often make their greatest poets **generals**?
δικαστῇ χρώμεθα τῷ Διονύσῳ. = Let us use Dionysus **[as] a judge**.

§ 189 Definite article without a noun to create a substantive
- The case, number, and gender of the definite article allow inference of the missing noun.
- accompanying an adjective being used substantively (§124)

οἱ πολλοί = the many
τοὺς μώρους = the foolish

- accompanying a participle being used substantively (§169)

τὰ γενόμενα = the things that happened, past events
ὁ τρέχων = the running man
αἱ διὰ τῆς ἀγορᾶς ἐλθοῦσαι = the women who went through the agora
οἱ τὴν πόλιν φυλάττοντες = those guarding the city, those who guard the city
οἱ εὖ λέγοντες κρείττονές εἰσι **τῶν εὖ μαχομένων**. = **Those who speak well** are stronger than **those who fight well**.

- with no noun, adjective, or participle expressed, but accompanied by a prepositional phrase, adverb, or the like

  οἱ ἐν τῇ νήσῳ τοὺς βαρβάρους φοβοῦνται. = **Those on the island** fear the barbarians.

  contrast: τοὺς **ἐν τῇ νήσῳ** βαρβάρους φοβοῦνται. = They fear the barbarians **[who are] on the island**. [note the importance of the definite article in these two examples for correct understanding of the phrase *on the island*]

  τὰ **τῶν τότε** ἔργα μείζονα ἢ τὰ **τῶν νῦν**. = The deeds **of those then** [are] greater than the [deeds] **of those now**. *or* The deeds **of past people** [are] greater than the [deeds] **of our contemporaries**.

  ὁ Ἀριστόδημος Σωκράτους ἐραστὴς ἦν ἐν **τοῖς μάλιστα τῶν τότε**. = Aristodemus was a lover of Socrates among **those who [were] particularly [so] of those at that time**. *or* Aristodemus was among **the particularly passionate lovers** of Socrates **of that time**.

§ 190 Definite article with no noun or adjective expressed, accompanying μέν … δέ

- translate: "one … the other [singular] *or* some … the others [plural]"
- Case and gender of the definite article contributes to the translation.

  οἱ μὲν λέγουσι, **οἱ δὲ** σιωπῶσιν. = **Some** speak, **the others** are silent.
  ὁ μὲν φεύγει, **ὁ δὲ** διώκει. = **One man** flees, **the other** chases.
  τοὺς ἄνδρας **αἱ μὲν** φιλοῦσι, **αἱ δὲ** μισοῦσι. = **Some of the women** love their husbands, **the others** hate [them].
  τοὺς μὲν φιλοῦμεν, **τοὺς δὲ** μισοῦμεν. = We love **some of the men**, we hate **the others**.

- Definite articles need not match in case, number, or gender.

  τὰ μὲν ἐκφευξόμεθα, **τῶν δὲ** τευξόμεθα. = We will avoid **some things**, and will obtain **others**.

- One element may be singled out from a group using the definite article + μέν … δέ.

  οἱ μὲν τοὺς λόγους αὐτοῦ ἐπήνουν, **ὁ δὲ Ἀριστοφάνης** λέγειν τι ἐπεχείρει. = **The others** praised his words, **but Aristophanes** was trying to say something.

§ 191 Definite article before αὐτός -ή -ό

- translate: "the same"

  τὸ αὐτὸ πάθος ἐπάθομεν. = We endured **the same** experience.

τὴν αὐτὴν φωνὴν ἐφωνοῦμεν. = We spoke **the same** language.

οἱ αὐτοὶ ταύτῃ τῇ συνουσίᾳ παρεγένοντο. = **The same men** were present at this gathering.

Miscellanea

Uses of ὡς (§§192–199)

§ 192 Ὡς + indicative (or participle)
- translate: "as, when, since, because"
- with indicative

> ὡς αἱ ψυχαὶ ἐπὶ τὸ πέδιον ἀφίκοντο, ἑκάστη ἔπιε μέτρον τι τοῦ ὕδατος. = **As** the souls arrived on the plain, each drank some portion of the water. *or* **When** the souls arrived on the plain, each drank some portion of the water.
> ὡς οὐχ οἷοί τ᾽ ἐσμὲν ἐλθεῖν οἴκαδε, μενοῦμεν ἐνθάδε. = **As** we are not able to go home, we will wait here. *or* **Because** we are not able to go home, we will remain here.

- particularly common in brief parenthetical statements

> ὡς οἶμαι = as I think
> ὡς ἔοικε = as it seems
> ὡς ἐμοὶ δοκεῖ = as it seems to me, as seems good to me
> ὡς δεῖ = as is necessary
> ὡς ἄρτι ἔλεγον = as I was just saying

- with participle

> ὀργίζονται **ὡς ἀδικούμενοι**. = They are angry **because of being treated unjustly**. *or* They are angry **because they are being treated unjustly**.
> ἔλαβον δίκην παρὰ αὐτοῦ **ὡς ἀδικοῦντος**. = They punished him **on the grounds of his acting unjustly**. *or* They punished him **because he was acting unjustly**.

§ 193 Ὡς in exclamations
- followed by an adjective or adverb
- translate: "how . . . !"

> **ὡς ἡδέως** λέγεις. = **How sweetly** you speak!
> **ὡς καλὴ** ἡ ἀκρόπολις. = **How beautiful** is the acropolis!

§ 194 Ὡς in indirect statements

- with main verb of speaking, thinking, knowing (= ὅτι)
- translate: "that"

εἶπεν **ὡς** οὐκ εἰδείη οὐδέν. = He said **that** he did not know anything.

§ 195 Ὡς in indirect questions

- with main verb of asking or similar (= πῶς, ὅπως)
- translate: "how"

ἤρετο **ὡς** Σωκράτης καταδικασθείη. = He asked **how** Socrates had been convicted.

§ 196 Ὡς + future participle

- translate: "with the intention of —— ing *or* in order to —— *or* to ——"

ἔβησαν ἐκεῖσε **ὡς πιόμενοι** τὸ ὕδωρ. = They went there **to drink** the water.

§ 197 Ὡς + subjunctive or optative[9]

- to create a purpose clause
- translate: "in order that *or* so that *or* in order to" (= ὅπως, ἵνα)

εἴθε γενοίμην οὐρανός, **ὡς** πολλοῖς ὄμμασιν εἰς σὲ **βλέπω.** = If only I could become the sky, **so that I could look** at you with many eyes.

§ 198 Ὡς + superlative adjective or adverb

- translate: "as —— as possible"

ὡς τάχιστα ἴωμεν. = Let us go **as quickly as possible**.

§ 199 Ὡς + accusative of person

- translate: "to *accusative's* house"

οὗτοι ἔδραμον **ὡς** Σωκράτη. = These men ran **to Socrates' house**.

Uses of αὐτός (§§200–205)

§ 200 Αὐτός in nominative to emphasize the subject

- In the nominative, αὐτός always intensifies the subject of the verb, whatever it might be, yielding many different translations: I myself, you yourself, he himself, etc.

---

9. Optative is normally used to replace a subjunctive after a main verb in the past (§159b).

ἔθυεν **αὐτός** τε καὶ οἱ χορευταί. = **He himself** was sacrificing—as were his chorus members.

θαυμάζω καὶ **αὐτός**. = **I myself** also wonder.

ἥδομαί τινας περὶ φιλοσοφίας λόγους **αὐτὸς** ποιούμενος ἢ ἄλλων ἀκούων. = **I** enjoy making certain speeches about philosophy **myself** or listening to others [make them]. [Greek word order allows the meaning to emerge more naturally than this English translation]

§ 201 Αὐτός alone, not in the nominative, as third-person pronoun

* Alone in the oblique cases (all but nominative), αὐτός serves as a third personal pronoun.
* translate: "him, her, it, them," etc.

ἑταῖρος Σωκράτους ὤν, δικαιότατος εἶ τοὺς λόγους **αὐτοῦ** ἀπαγγέλλειν. = Being Socrates' companion, you are the best person to publicize **his** words.

ἐᾶτε **αὐτόν**. = Leave **him** be.

§ 202 Αὐτός in predicate position to emphasize nouns and pronouns

* Accompanying another noun or pronoun in any case in the predicate position (§123), αὐτός intensifies that noun or pronoun.

τὸν θεὸν αὐτόν = the god himself
ὑμᾶς αὐτούς = you yourselves
Σωκρατὴς αὐτός = Socrates himself
τοῦτο αὐτό = this very thing

§ 203 ὁ (definite article) + αὐτός = "the same"

τὸν αὐτὸν θεόν = the same god
ὁ αὐτός = the same man
τὰς αὐτάς = the same women
τῇ αὐτῇ ἡμέρᾳ = on the same day
ἐν τῷ αὐτῷ = in the same [place]
Σωκράτης ἀεὶ διὰ **τῶν αὐτῶν τὰ αὐτὰ** φαίνεται λέγειν. = Socrates always seems to be saying **the same things** through **the same things** [i.e., examples, images, or similar].

§ 204 Definite article + αὐτός in crasis (§207)

αὐτή = ἡ αὐτή = the same woman [the combination of rough breathing and acute on ultima distinguishes from αὕτη (from οὗτος) and from αὐτή (from αὐτός)]
ταὐτό(ν) = τὸ αὐτό = the same thing

§ 205 With a rough breathing (αὑτόν), αὑτός is contracted from reflexive ἑαυτόν (himself)

ἐγὼ τὴν ἡμετέρην τέχνην τιμήσω ὥσπερ Ἐρυξίμαχος τὴν **αὑτοῦ**. = I will honor our art, just as Eryximachus [did] **his**.

Other

§ 206 Anastrophe

- Anastrophe results when a preposition that is normally accented on the final syllable (e.g., ἀνά, ἀπό, διά, παρά, περί) is accented instead on the first syllable. This signals that the object of the preposition precedes the preposition rather than following it, as it normally does.

οἴονται ἀθάνατον μνήμην **ἀρετῆς πέρι** ἑαυτῶν ἔσεσθαι. = They think that there will be a lasting memorial of them **for virtue**.

§ 207 Crasis

- The blending of two words, crasis can occur when one word ends in a vowel and the word immediately following begins with a vowel. Although more common in poetry than prose, common words may be joined through crasis in Attic prose. It can often be recognized by a breathing mark in a word beginning with a consonant or by some other change in the normal accentuation of a word.

κἀγώ = καὶ ἐγώ
αὑτή = ἡ αὐτή [distinguish from αὐτή and demonstrative adjective αὕτη]
κἀμοῦ = καὶ ἐμοῦ
ἅνθρωποι = οἱ ἄνθρωποι
κἂν = καὶ ἔαν or καὶ ἄν
ὠγαθέ = ὦ ἀγαθέ
ταὐτό(ν) = τὸ αὐτό [the addition of ν to ταὐτό is common in Attic]

§ 208 Prolepsis (anticipation)

- Prolepsis (anticipation) is a common phenomenon in Greek whereby the subject of a dependent clause is *anticipated* by being made part of the main clause.

βούλομαι δὲ μάλιστα πυθέσθαι **περὶ τῶν ἐρωτικῶν λόγων τίνες** ἦσαν. = I wish very much to learn **what the erotic speeches** were. *or more literally* I wish very much to learn **about the erotic speeches what they** were.

τοῦτον τὸν νεανίαν οὐκ οἶδα τίς ἐστίν. = I don't know **who this young man** is. *or more literally* I don't know **this young man who he** is.

φοβοῦμαι **αὐτὴν μή** τι βουλεύσῃ κακόν. = I fear **that she** will plan something bad. *or more literally* I fear **her lest she** plan something bad.

τὸ καλὸν ὁρᾷ **ὅτι πᾶν αὐτὸ** αὑτῷ συγγενές ἐστιν. = He sees **that all the beautiful itself** is related to itself. *or more literally* He sees **the beautiful that it all itself** is related to itself.

πρῶτον μὲν δεῖ **αὐτὸν** ἐπιδεῖξαι ὁποῖός τίς ἐστιν ὁ Ἔρως, ὕστερον δὲ τὰ ἔργα αὐτοῦ. = It is necessary to show first what sort of a being Eros **himself** is; second, [to show] his achievements. *or more literally* First, it is necessary to show **himself** what sort of a being Eros is; second, [to show] his achievements.

Prolepsis is sometimes called "the lilies of the field construction," based on the famous biblical verse: "Consider the lilies of the field, how they grow" (Matthew 6.28). This translation preserves the Greek prolepsis rather than using the more conventional English practice: "Consider how the lilies of the field grow."

Appendix: 247 Common Attic Verbs and Their Principal Parts

Key to appendix

-      a hyphen before a principal part indicates that the form is found only with a prefix

[ ]   square brackets enclose a prefix; verbs with prefixes may occur more rarely without the prefix

( )   parentheses enclose (1) stems not necessarily predictable from the part or (2) individual letters that are sometimes omitted

{ }   curly braces enclose prefixed forms that are particularly common in Attic

—   an em dash indicates a form not found in Attic Greek

*   an asterisk indicates a form taken from another verb with the same meaning

/   a solidus separates alternative forms

present	basic meaning	future	aorist	perfect	perfect middle-passive	aorist passive
ἀγαπάω	love	ἀγαπήσω	ἠγάπησα	ἠγάπηκα	ἠγάπημαι	ἠγαπήθην
ἀγγέλλω	announce	ἀγγελῶ	ἤγγειλα	ἤγγελκα	ἤγγελμαι	ἠγγέλθην
ἀγνοέω	be ignorant	ἀγνοήσω	ἠγνόησα	ἠγνόηκα	ἠγνόημαι	ἠγνοήθην
ἄγω	lead	ἄξω	ἤγαγον	ἦχα	ἦγμαι	ἤχθην
ἀδικέω	do wrong	ἀδικήσω	ἠδίκησα	ἠδίκηκα	ἠδίκημαι	ἠδικήθην
ᾄδω	sing	ᾄσομαι	ᾖσα	—	ᾖσμαι	ᾔσθην
αἰνέω {ἐπαινέω}	praise	-αινέσω/ -αινέσομαι	-ήνεσα	-ήνεκα	-ήνημαι	-ηνέθην
αἱρέω	take, capture; mid.: choose	αἱρήσω	εἷλον (ἑλ-)	ᾕρηκα	ᾕρημαι	ᾑρέθην
αἴρω	lift	ἀρῶ	ἦρα	ἦρκα	ἦρμαι	ἤρθην
αἰσθάνομαι	perceive	αἰσθήσομαι	ᾐσθόμην	—	ᾔσθημαι	—
αἰσχύνω	shame; mid.: feel shame	αἰσχυνῶ	ᾔσχυνα	—	—	ᾐσχύνθην
αἰτέω	ask	αἰτήσω	ᾔτησα	ᾔτηκα	ᾔτημαι	ᾐτήθην
ἀκούω	hear	ἀκούσομαι	ἤκουσα	ἀκήκοα	—	ἠκούσθην
ἁλίσκομαι	be caught	ἁλώσομαι	ἑάλων/ἥλων	ἑάλωκα/ἥλωκα	—	—
ἀλλάττω	change, exchange	ἀλλάξω	ἤλλαξα	-ήλλαχα	ἤλλαγμαι	ἠλλάχθην/ ἠλλάγην
ἁμαρτάνω	err, do wrong, miss	ἁμαρτήσομαι	ἥμαρτον	ἡμάρτηκα	ἡμάρτημαι	ἡμαρτήθην
ἀμελέω	not care	ἀμελήσω	ἠμέλησα	ἠμέληκα	ἠμέλημαι	ἠμελήθην
ἀμύνω	ward off; mid.: defend oneself	ἀμυνῶ	ἤμυνα	—	—	—
ἀναγκάζω	force, compel	ἀναγκάσω	ἠνάγκασα	ἠνάγκακα	ἠνάγκασμαι	ἠναγκάσθην
[ἀνα]λίσκω	spend	ἀναλώσω	ἀνάλωσα/ ἀνήλωσα	ἀνάλωκα/ ἀνήλωκα	ἀνάλωμαι/ ἀνήλωμαι	ἀναλώθην/ ἀνηλώθην
[ἀν]οίγνυμι/ [ἀν]οίγω	open	ἀνοίξω	ἀνέῳξα	ἀνέῳχα	ἀνέῳγμαι	ἀνεῴχθην

present	basic meaning	future	aorist	perfect	perfect middle-passive	aorist passive
ἀξιόω	deem worthy	ἀξιώσω	ἠξίωσα	ἠξίωκα	ἠξίωμαι	ἠξιώθην
[ἀπ]αντάω	meet	ἀπαντήσομαι	ἀπήντησα	ἀπήντηκα	—	—
ἀπατάω {ἐξαπατάω}	deceive	ἀπατήσω	ἠπάτησα	ἠπάτηκα	ἠπάτημαι	ἠπατήθην
[ἀπο]κρίνομαι	answer	ἀποκρινοῦμαι	ἀπεκρινάμην	—	ἀποκέκριμαι	—
[ἀπ]όλλυμι	destroy; *mid.*: perish	ἀπολῶ	ἀπώλεσα; *mid.*: ἀπωλόμην	ἀπόλωλεκα/ ἀπόλωλα ["I am ruined"]	—	—
[ἀπο]λογέομαι	speak in defense	ἀπολογήσομαι	ἀπελογησάμην	—	ἀπολελόγημαι	—
ἀπορέω	be at a loss	ἀπορήσω	ἠπόρησα	ἠπόρηκα	ἠπόρημαι	ἠπορήθην
ἅπτω	light, fasten; *mid.*: touch	ἅψω	ἧψα	—	ἧμμαι	ἥφθην
ἀρέσκω	please	ἀρέσω	ἤρεσα	—	—	ἠρέσθην
ἁρπάζω	seize	ἁρπάσομαι/ ἁρπάσω	ἥρπασα	ἥρπακα	ἥρπασμαι	ἡρπάσθην
ἄρχω	rule; *mid.*: begin	ἄρξω	ἦρξα	ἦρχα	ἦργμαι	ἤρχθην
ἀτιμάζω	dishonor	ἀτιμάσω	ἠτίμασα	ἠτίμακα	ἠτίμασμαι	ἠτιμάσθην
αὔξω/αὐξάνω	increase, grow	αὐξήσω	ηὔξησα	ηὔξηκα	ηὔξημαι	ηὐξήθην
[ἀφ]ικνέομαι	arrive	ἀφίξομαι	ἀφικόμην	—	ἀφῖγμαι	—
βαδίζω	walk	βαδιοῦμαι	ἐβάδισα	βεβάδικα	—	—
βαίνω	go	-βήσομαι	-ἔβην (β-) (root aorist; §64)	βέβηκα	-βέβαμαι	-ἐβάθην
βάλλω	throw	βαλῶ	ἔβαλον	βέβληκα	βέβλημαι	ἐβλήθην
βλάπτω	harm	βλάψω	ἔβλαψα	βέβλαφα	βέβλαμμαι	ἐβλάβην/ ἐβλάφθην
βλέπω	look	βλέψομαι	ἔβλεψα	βέβλεφα	βέβλεμμαι	ἐβλέφθην
βοάω	shout	βοήσομαι	ἐβόησα	—	—	—
βοηθέω	help, rescue	βοηθήσομαι	ἐβοήθησα	βεβοήθηκα	βεβοήθημαι	ἐβοηθήθην

present	basic meaning	future	aorist	perfect	perfect middle-passive	aorist passive
βουλεύω	counsel, advise	βουλεύσω	ἐβούλευσα	βεβούλευκα	βεβούλευμαι	ἐβουλεύθην
βούλομαι	wish	βουλήσομαι	—	—	βεβούλημαι	ἐβουλήθην
γαμέω	marry	γαμῶ	ἔγημα	γεγάμηκα	γεγάμημαι	—
γελάω	laugh	γελάσομαι	ἐγέλασα	—	—	ἐγελάσθην
γεννάω	beget	γεννήσω	ἐγέννησα	γεγέννηκα	γεγέννημαι	ἐγεννήθην
γίγνομαι	become, arise, happen, be	γενήσομαι	ἐγενόμην	γέγονα	γεγένημαι	ἐγενήθην
γιγνώσκω	know, recognize	γνώσομαι	ἔγνων (γν-) (root aorist; §64)	ἔγνωκα	ἔγνωσμαι	ἐγνώσθην
γράφω	write	γράψω	ἔγραψα	γέγραφα	γέγραμμαι	ἐγράφην
γυμνάζω	train, exercise	γυμνάσω	ἐγύμνασα	γεγύμνακα	γεγύμνασμαι	ἐγυμνάσθην
δάκνω	bite	δήξομαι	ἔδακον	—	δέδηγμαι	ἐδήχθην
δείδω	fear	δείσομαι	ἔδεισα	δέδοικα/δέδια	—	—
δείκνυμι	show	δείξω	ἔδειξα	δέδειχα	δέδειγμαι	ἐδείχθην
δειπνέω	dine	δειπνήσω	ἐδείπνησα	δεδείπνηκα	δεδείπνημαι	ἐδειπνήθην
δέχομαι	receive	δέξομαι	ἐδεξάμην	—	δέδεγμαι	—
δέω (1)	bind	δήσω	ἔδησα	δέδεκα	δέδεμαι	ἐδέθην
δέω (2)	need; mid.: want, ask for	δεήσω	ἐδέησα	δεδέηκα	δεδέημαι	ἐδεήθην
δηλόω	show, reveal	δηλώσω	ἐδήλωσα	δεδήλωκα	δεδήλωμαι	ἐδηλώθην
[δια]λέγομαι	converse	διαλέξομαι	—	—	διείλεγμαι	διελέχθην/διαλέγην
[δια]νοέομαι	think over	διανοήσομαι	—	—	διανενόημαι	διενοήθην
[δια]φθείρω	ruin, destroy, corrupt	διαφθερῶ	διέφθειρα	διέφθαρκα/διέφθορα	διέφθαρμαι	διεφθάρην
διδάσκω	teach	διδάξω	ἐδίδαξα	δεδίδαχα	δεδίδαγμαι	ἐδιδάχθην
δίδωμι	give	δώσω	ἔδωκα (δο-) (§62)	δέδωκα	δέδομαι	ἐδόθην
[δι]ηγέομαι	narrate, describe	διηγήσομαι	διηγησάμην	—	διήγημαι	—

present	basic meaning	future	aorist	perfect	perfect middle–passive	aorist passive
δικάζω	judge	δικάσω	ἐδίκασα	δεδίκακα	δεδίκασμαι	ἐδικάσθην
διώκω	pursue	διώξομαι/ διώξω	ἐδίωξα	δεδίωχα	δεδίωγμαι	ἐδιώχθην
δοκέω	seem	δόξω	ἔδοξα	—	δέδογμαι	-εδόχθην
δουλεύω	serve, be a slave	δουλεύσω	ἐδούλευσα	δεδούλευκα	δεδούλευμαι	ἐδουλεύθην
δράω	do	δράσω	ἔδρασα	δέδρακα	δέδραμαι	ἐδράσθην
δύναμαι	be able	δυνήσομαι	—	—	δεδύνημαι	ἐδυνήθην
ἐάω	allow	ἐάσω	εἴασα	εἴακα	εἴαμαι	εἰάθην
ἐγείρω	rouse	ἐγερῶ	ἤγειρα/ἠγρόμην	ἐγρήγορα	ἐγήγερμαι	ἠγέρθην
ἐθέλω	wish, want	ἐθελήσω	ἠθέλησα	ἠθέληκα	—	—
εἰκάζω	make like, compare	εἰκάσω	ᾔκασα	—	ᾔκασμαι	ᾐκάσθην
εἰμί (§65)	be	ἔσομαι (§66)	—	—	—	—
[ἐκ]πλήττω	scare	ἐκπλήξω	ἐξέπληξα	ἐκπέπληγα	ἐκπέπληγμαι	ἐξεπλάγην/ ἐξεπλήγην
ἐλαύνω	drive	ἐλάω	ἤλασα	-ἐλήλακα	ἐλήλαμαι	ἠλάθην
ἐλέγχω	examine, prove	ἐλέγξω	ἤλεγξα	—	ἐλήλεγμαι	ἠλέγχθην
ἐλεέω	pity	ἐλεήσω	ἠλέησα	ἠλέηκα	ἠλέημαι	ἠλεήθην
ἕλκω	draw	-έλξω	εἵλκυσα	-είλκυκα	-εἵλκυσμαι	εἱλκύσθην
ἐλπίζω	hope	ἐλπιῶ	ἤλπισα	—	—	ἠλπίσθην
[ἐπι]θυμέω	desire	ἐπιθυμήσω	ἐπεθύμησα	ἐπιτεθύμηκα	—	ἐπεθυμήθην
[ἐπι]μελ(έ)ομαι	care for	ἐπιμελήσομαι	—	—	ἐπιμεμέλημαι	ἐπεμελήθην
ἐπίσταμαι	know	ἐπιστήσομαι	—	—	—	ἠπιστήθην
[ἐπι]τηδεύω	pursue	ἐπιτηδεύσω	ἐπετήδευσα	ἐπιτετήδευκα	ἐπιτετήδευμαι	ἐπετηδεύθην
[ἐπι]χειρέω	try, attack	ἐπιχειρήσω	ἐπεχείρησα	ἐπικεχείρηκα	ἐπικεχείρημαι	ἐπεχειρήθην
ἕπομαι	follow	ἕψομαι	ἑσπόμην	—	—	—
ἐράω	love, desire	ἐρασθήσομαι	—	—	—	ἠράσθην
ἐργάζομαι	work, do	ἐργάσομαι	ἠργασάμην	—	εἴργασμαι	ἠργάσθην

present	basic meaning	future	aorist	perfect	perfect middle-passive	aorist passive
ἔρχομαι	go, come	*εἶμι (§66) / ἐλεύσομαι	ἦλθον (ἐλθ-)	ἐλήλυθα	—	—
ἐρωτάω	ask	ἐρωτήσω / *ἐρήσομαι	ἠρώτησα / *ἠρόμην	ἠρώτηκα	ἠρώτημαι	ἠρωτήθην
ἐσθίω	eat	ἔδομαι	*ἔφαγον	ἐδήδοκα	-ἐδήδεσμαι	ἠδέσθην
εὐλαβέομαι	take care	εὐλαβήσομαι	—	—	—	ηὐλαβήθην
εὑρίσκω	find	εὑρήσω	ηὗρον/εὗρον	ηὕρηκα/εὕρηκα	ηὕρημαι/εὕρημαι	ηὑρέθην
εὔχομαι	pray, boast	εὔξομαι	ηὐξάμην	—	ηὖγμαι	—
ἔχω	have, hold	ἕξω/σχήσω	ἔσχον (σχ-)	ἔσχηκα	-ἔσχημαι	ἐσχέθην
ζάω	live	ζήσω	—	—	—	—
ζηλόω	envy	ζηλώσω	ἐζήλωσα	ἐζήλωκα	ἐζήλωμαι	ἐζηλώθην
ζητέω	seek	ζητήσω	ἐζήτησα	ἐζήτηκα	ἐζήτημαι	ἐζητήθην
ἡγέομαι	lead, consider	ἡγήσομαι	ἡγησάμην	—	ἥγημαι	-ἡγήθην
ἥδομαι	enjoy	ἡσθήσομαι	—	—	—	ἥσθην
ἥκω	have come	ἥξω	—	—	—	—
ἡττάομαι	be less	ἡττήσομαι	—	—	ἥττημαι	ἡττήθην
θάπτω	bury	θάψω	ἔθαψα	—	τέθαμμαι	ἐτάφην
θαυμάζω	wonder	θαυμάσομαι	ἐθαύμασα	τεθαύμακα	τεθαύμασμαι	ἐθαυμάσθην
θεάομαι	watch	θεάσομαι	ἐθεασάμην	—	τεθέαμαι	—
θνῄσκω {ἀποθνῄσκω}	die	-θανοῦμαι	-έθανον	τέθνηκα	—	—
θύω	sacrifice	θύσω	ἔθυσα	τέθυκα	τέθυμαι	ἐτύθην
ἰάομαι	heal	ἰάσομαι	ἰασάμην	—	ἴαμαι	ἰάθην
ἵημι {ἀφίημι}	set going	ἥσω	-ἧκα (ἕ-) (§62)	-εἷκα	-εἷμαι	-εἵθην
ἵστημι	set, stand	στήσω	ἔστησα/ἔστην (root aorist; §64)	ἕστηκα (§63)	ἕσταμαι	ἐστάθην
[καθ]εύδω	sleep	καθευδήσω	—	—	—	—

present	basic meaning	future	aorist	perfect	perfect middle-passive	aorist passive
[καθ]ίζω	sit	καθιῶ	ἐκάθισα/καθῖσα	—	—	ἐκαύθην
καίω/κάω	burn	καύσω	ἔκαυσα	-κέκαυκα	κέκαυμαι	ἐκλήθην
καλέω	call	καλῶ	ἐκάλεσα	κέκληκα	κέκλημαι	—
κάμνω	toil	καμοῦμαι	ἔκαμον	κέκμηκα	—	—
[κατα]δαρθάνω	sleep	—	κατέδαρθον	καταδεδάρθηκα	—	—
κεῖμαι	lie	κείσομαι	—	—	—	ἐκελεύσθην
κελεύω	order, bid	κελεύσω	ἐκέλευσα	κεκέλευκα	κεκέλευσμαι	ἐκινδυνεύθην
κινδυνεύω	risk	κινδυνεύσω	ἐκινδύνευσα	κεκινδύνευκα	κεκινδύνευμαι	ἐκινήθην
κινέω	move	κινήσω	ἐκίνησα	κεκίνηκα	κεκίνημαι	—
κλάω/κλαίω	weep	κλαήσω/κλαιήσω	ἔκλαυσα	—	κέκλαυμαι/κέκλαυσμαι	ἐκλάπην/ἐκλέφθην
κλέπτω	steal	κλέψω	ἔκλεψα	κέκλοφα	κέκλεμμαι	-εκλίνην/ἐκλίθην
κλίνω	bend, incline, recline	κλινῶ	ἔκλινα	κέκλικα	κέκλιμαι	ἐκολάσθην
κολάζω	punish	κολάσω	ἐκόλασα	—	κεκόλασμαι	ἐκομίσθην
κομίζω	care for, carry	κομιῶ	ἐκόμισα	κεκόμικα	κεκόμισμαι	-εκόπην
κόπτω	strike	κόψω	ἔκοψα	-κέκοφα	κέκομμαι	ἐκρατήθην
κρατέω	rule	κρατήσω	ἐκράτησα	κεκράτηκα	κεκράτημαι	ἐκρίθην
κρίνω	judge	κρινῶ	ἔκρινα	κέκρικα	κέκριμαι	ἐκρύφθην
κρύπτω	hide	κρύψω	ἔκρυψα	—	κέκρυμμαι	ἐκτήθην
κτάομαι	acquire	κτήσομαι	ἐκτησάμην	—	κέκτημαι	—
κτείνω {ἀποκτείνω}	kill	κτενῶ	ἔκτεινα	-έκτονα	—	ἐκωλύθην
κωλύω	hinder	κωλύσω	ἐκώλυσα	κεκώλυκα	κεκώλυμαι	ἐλήχθην
λαγχάνω	obtain by lot	λήξομαι	ἔλαχον	εἴληχα	εἴληγμαι	—

present	basic meaning	future	aorist	perfect	perfect middle-passive	aorist passive
λαμβάνω	take	λήψομαι	ἔλαβον	εἴληφα	εἴλημμαι	ἐλήφθην
λανθάνω	escape the notice of	λήσω	ἔλαθον	λέληθα	-λέλησμαι	—
λέγω	say, speak, tell	*ἐρῶ/λέξω	*εἶπον/ἔλεξα	*εἴρηκα	*εἴρημαι/λέλεγμαι	*ἐρρήθην/ἐλέχθην
λείπω	leave	λείψω	ἔλιπον	λέλοιπα	λέλειμμαι	ἐλείφθην
λήγω	cease	λήξω	ἔληξα	—	—	—
λύω	release	λύσω	ἔλυσα	λέλυκα	λέλυμαι	ἐλύθην
μαίνομαι	rage, run mad	μανοῦμαι	ἐμηνάμην	μέμηνα (with present meaning)	μεμάνημαι	ἐμάνην
μανθάνω	learn	μαθήσομαι	ἔμαθον	μεμάθηκα	—	—
μαντεύομαι	prophesy	μαντεύσομαι	ἐμαντευσάμην	—	μεμάντευμαι	—
μάχομαι	fight	μαχοῦμαι	ἐμαχεσάμην	—	μεμάχημαι	—
μείγνυμι/ μίγνυμι	mix	μείξω	ἔμειξα	—	μεμείγμαι	ἐμείχθην
μέλλω	be about to	μελλήσω	ἐμέλλησα	—	—	—
μέλω	be a concern	μελήσω	ἐμέλησα	μεμέληκα	—	—
μέμφομαι	blame	μέμψομαι	ἐμεμψάμην	—	—	ἐμέμφθην
μένω	wait	μενῶ	ἔμεινα	μεμένηκα	—	—
μηχανάομαι	devise	μηχανήσομαι	ἐμηχανησάμην	—	μεμηχάνημαι	—
μιμνῄσκω	remind	μνήσω	ἔμνησα	-μέμνηκα	μέμνημαι	ἐμνήσθην
νέμω	distribute	νεμῶ	ἔνειμα	-νενέμηκα	νενέμημαι	ἐνεμήθην
νικάω	win, conquer	νικήσω	ἐνίκησα	νενίκηκα	νενίκημαι	ἐνικήθην
νοέω	think, perceive	νοήσω	ἐνόησα	νενόηκα	νενόημαι	ἐνοήθην
νομίζω	believe	νομιῶ	ἐνόμισα	νενόμικα	νενόμισμαι	ἐνομίσθην
οἶδα (§65)	know	εἴσομαι	—	—	—	—
οἰκέω	live	οἰκήσω	ᾤκησα	ᾤκηκα	ᾤκημαι	ᾠκήθην
οἰκτ(ε)ίρω	pity	οἰκτιρῶ	ᾤκτ(ε)ιρα	—	—	—

present	basic meaning	future	aorist	perfect	perfect middle-passive	aorist passive
οἴομαι/οἶμαι	think	οἰήσομαι	—	—	—	ᾠήθην
οἴχομαι	be gone	οἰχήσομαι	—	—	—	—
ὄμνυμι	swear	ὀμοῦμαι	ὤμοσα	ὀμώμοκα	ὀμώμο(σ)μαι	ὠμό(σ)θην
ὁμολογέω	agree	ὁμολογήσω	ὡμολόγησα	ὡμολόγηκα	ὡμολόγημαι	ὡμολογήθην
ὀνειδίζω	reproach	ὀνειδιῶ	ὠνείδισα	ὠνείδικα	—	ὠνειδίσθην
ὀνομάζω	name	ὀνομάσω	ὠνόμασα	ὠνόμακα	ὠνόμασμαι	ὠνομάσθην
ὁράω	see	ὄψομαι	εἶδον (ἰδ-)	ἑόρακα/ἑώρακα	ἑόραμαι/ὦμμαι	ὤφθην
ὀργίζω	anger	ὀργιῶ	ὤργισα	—	ὤργισμαι	ὠργίσθην
ὁρμάω	rouse	ὁρμήσω	ὥρμησα	ὥρμηκα	ὥρμημαι	ὡρμήθην
ὀφείλω	owe	ὀφειλήσω	ὠφείλησα/ ὤφελον	ὠφείληκα	—	ὠφειλήθην
παιδεύω	educate	παιδεύσω	ἐπαίδευσα	πεπαίδευκα	πεπαίδευμαι	ἐπαιδεύθην
παίζω	play, tease	παίσομαι	ἔπαισα	πέπαικα	πέπαισμαι	—
[παρα]σκευάζω	prepare	παρασκευάσω	παρεσκεύασα	παρεσκεύακα	παρεσκεύασμαι	παρεσκευάσθην
πάσχω	suffer	πείσομαι	ἔπαθον	πέπονθα	—	—
παύω	stop	παύσω	ἔπαυσα	πέπαυκα	πέπαυμαι	ἐπαύ(σ)θην
πείθω	persuade; mid.: trust, obey	πείσω	ἔπεισα/ἔπιθον	πέπεικα/πέποιθα	πέπεισμαι	ἐπείσθην
πειράω	try	πειράσω	ἐπείρασα	πεπείρακα	πεπείραμαι	ἐπειράθην
πέμπω	send	πέμψω	ἔπεμψα	πέπομφα	πέπεμμαι	ἐπέμφθην
πίμπλημι	fill	-πλήσω	-έπλησα	-πέπληκα	-πέπλημαι	-ἐπλήσθην
πίνω	drink	πίομαι	ἔπιον	πέπωκα	-πέπομαι	-ἐπόθην
πίπτω	throw	πεσοῦμαι	ἔπεσον	πέπτωκα	—	—
πιστεύω	trust	πιστεύσω	ἐπίστευσα	πεπίστευκα	πεπίστευμαι	ἐπιστεύθην
πλέκω	weave	πλέξω	ἔπλεξα	πέπλεχα	πέπλεγμαι	ἐπλέχθην/ ἐπλάκην/ ἐπλέχθην
πλέω	sail	πλεύσομαι	ἔπλευσα	πέπλευκα	πέπλευσμαι	

115

present	basic meaning	future	aorist	perfect	perfect middle-passive	aorist passive
ποιέω	do, make	ποιήσω	ἐποίησα	πεποίηκα	πεποίημαι	ἐποιήθην
πορεύομαι	travel	πορεύσομαι	-επορευσάμην	—	πεπόρευμαι	ἐπορεύθην
πορίζω	provide; mid.: procure	ποριῶ	ἐπόρισα	πεπόρικα	πεπόρισμαι	ἐπορίσθην
πράττω	do	πράξω	ἔπραξα	πέπραχα/πέπραγα	πέπραγμαι	ἐπράχθην
πυνθάνομαι	learn, inquire	πεύσομαι	ἐπυθόμην	—	πέπυσμαι	—
πωλέω	buy	πωλήσω	ἐπώλησα/*ἀπεδόμην	πεπώληκα/*πέπρακα	πεπώλημαι/*πέπραμαι	ἐπωλήθην/*ἐπράθην
ῥέω	flow	ῥυήσομαι	—	ἐρρύηκα	—	ἐρρύην
ῥήγνυμι	break	ῥήξω	ἔρρηξα	-έρρωγα	—	ἐρράγην
ῥίπτω	throw	ῥίψω	ἔρριψα	ἔρριφα	ἔρριμμαι	ἐρρίφ(θ)ην
σημαίνω	signal	σημανῶ	ἐσήμηνα	σεσήμαγκα	σεσήμασμαι	ἐσημάνθην
σιγάω	be silent	σιγήσομαι	ἐσίγησα	σεσίγηκα	σεσίγημαι	ἐσιγήθην
σκεδάννυμι	scatter	-σκεδάω	-εσκέδασα	—	ἐσκέδασμαι	ἐσκεδάσθην
σκέπτομαι/ σκοπέω	view	σκέψομαι	ἐσκεψάμην	—	ἔσκεμμαι	—
σπεύδω	hasten	σπεύσω	ἔσπευσα	—	—	ἐσπουδάσθην
σπουδάζω	be eager	σπουδάσομαι	ἐσπούδασα	ἐσπούδακα	ἐσπούδασμαι	ἐσπουδάσθην
στέλλω	send	στελῶ	ἔστειλα	-έσταλκα	ἔσταλμαι	ἐστάλην
στρέφω	turn, twist	στρέψω	ἔστρεψα	—	ἔστραμμαι	ἐστρέφθην/ ἐστράφην
[συλλέγω]	gather	συλλέξω	συνέλεξα	συνείλοχα	συνείλεγμαι	συνελέγην/ συνελέχθην
σῴζω	save	σώσω/σῴσω	ἔσωσα/ἔσῳσα	σέσωκα	σέσωμαι/ σέσῳσμαι	ἐσώθην
σωφρονέω	be moderate, exercise self-control	σωφρονήσω	ἐσωφρόνησα	σεσωφρόνηκα	σεσωφρόνημαι	—

present	basic meaning	future	aorist	perfect	perfect middle-passive	aorist passive
τάττω	arrange	τάξω	ἔταξα	τέταχα	τέταγμαι	ἐτάχθην
τείνω	stretch, extend	τενῶ	ἔτεινα	τέτακα	τέταμαι	ἐτάθην
τελευτάω	end	τελευτήσω	ἐτελεύτησα	τετελεύτηκα	τετελεύτημαι	ἐτελευτήθην
τέμνω	cut	τεμῶ	ἔτεμον	-τέτμηκα	τέτμημαι	ἐτμήθην
τίθημι	put, place	θήσω	ἔθηκα (θε-) (§62)	τέθηκα	τέθειμαι	ἐτέθην
τίκτω	bear, produce, give birth to	τέξομαι	ἔτεκον	τέτοκα	—	—
τιμάω	honor	τιμήσω	ἐτίμησα	τετίμηκα	τετίμημαι	ἐτιμήθην
τιμωρέω	avenge	τιμωρήσω	ἐτιμώρησα	τετιμώρηκα	τετιμώρημαι	ἐτιμωρήθην
τίνω	pay	τ(ε)ίσω	ἔτ(ε)ισα	τέτ(ε)ικα	-τέτεισμαι	-τ(ε)ίσθην
τιτρώσκω	wound	τρώσω	ἔτρωσα	—	τέτρωμαι	ἐτρώθην
τλάω	endure	τλήσομαι	ἔτλην (root aorist; §64)	τέτληκα	—	—
τολμάω	dare	τολμήσω	ἐτόλμησα	τετόλμηκα	τετόλμημαι	ἐτολμήθην
τρέπω	turn; mid.: flee	τρέψω	ἔτρεψα	τέτροφα	τέτραμμαι	ἐτράπην/ἐτρέφθην
τρέφω	nurse, nourish	θρέψω	ἔθρεψα	τέτροφα	τέθραμμαι	ἐτράφην/ἐθρέφθην
τρέχω	run	δραμοῦμαι	ἔδραμον	-δεδράμηκα	-δεδράμημαι	—
τρίβω	rub	τρίψω	ἔτριψα	τέτριφα	τέτριμμαι	ἐτρίβην
τυγχάνω	happen; obtain	τεύξομαι	ἔτυχον	τετύχηκα	—	—
τύπτω	strike	τυπτήσω	—	—	—	—
ὑβρίζω	wrong, harm	ὑβριῶ	ὕβρισα	ὕβρικα	ὕβρισμαι	ὑβρίσθην
ὑγιαίνω	be healthy	ὑγιανῶ	ὑγίανα	—	—	—
ὑμνέω	sing	ὑμνήσω	ὕμνησα	ὕμνηκα	ὕμνημαι	ὑμνήθην
ὑπισχνέομαι	promise	ὑποσχήσομαι	ὑπεσχόμην	—	ὑπέσχημαι	—

present	basic meaning	future	aorist	perfect	perfect middle-passive	aorist passive
[ὑπ]οπτεύω	suspect	ὑποπτεύσω	ὑπώπτευσα	—	—	ὑπωπτεύθην
φαίνω	show, appear	φανῶ	ἔφηνα	πέφηνα	πέφασμαι	ἐφάνην/ ἐφάνθην
φέρω	bear, carry	οἴσω	ἤνεγκα/ἤνεγκον	ἐνήνοχα	ἐνήνεγμαι	ἠνέχθην
φεύγω	flee	φεύξομαι	ἔφυγον	πέφευγα	—	—
φημί (§65)	say	φήσω	ἔφησα	—	—	—
φθάνω	anticipate	φθήσομαι	ἔφθασα/ἔφθην	—	—	—
φθείρω	corrupt	φθερῶ	ἔφθειρα	ἔφθαρκα/ -έφθορα	ἔφθαρμαι	ἐφθάρην
φιλέω	love	φιλήσω	ἐφίλησα	πεφίληκα	πεφίλημαι	ἐφιλήθην
φοβέομαι	fear	φοβήσομαι	—	—	πεφόβημαι	ἐφοβήθην
φράζω	tell, note	φράσω	ἔφρασα	πέφρακα	πέφρασμαι	ἐφράσθην
φρονέω	think	φρονήσω	ἐφρόνησα	πεφρόνηκα	πεφρόνημαι	ἐφρονήθην
φροντίζω	consider	φροντιῶ	ἐφρόντισα	πεφρόντικα	—	—
φυλάττω	guard	φυλάξω	ἐφύλαξα	πεφύλαχα	πεφύλαγμαι	ἐφυλάχθην
φύω	produce, grow	φύσω	ἔφυσα/ἔφυν	πέφυκα	—	ἐφύην
χαίρω	rejoice	χαιρήσω	—	κεχάρηκα	κεχάρη(η)μαι	ἐχάρην
χαρίζομαι	oblige, gratify	χαριοῦμαι	ἐχαρισάμην	—	κεχάρισμαι	—
χέω	pour	χέω	ἔχεα	κέχυκα	κέχυμαι	ἐχύθην
χράομαι	use, enjoy	χρήσομαι	ἐχρησάμην	—	κέχρημαι	ἐχρήσθην
χωρέω	give place, go	χωρήσω/ χωρήσομαι	ἐχώρησα	κεχώρηκα	κεχώρημαι	ἐχωρήθην
ψεύδομαι	lie, speak falsely	ψεύσομαι	ἐψευσάμην	—	ἔψευσμαι	ἐψεύσθην
ὠνέομαι	buy	ὠνήσομαι	*ἐπριάμην	—	ἐώνημαι	ἐωνήθην
ὠφελέω	help	ὠφελήσω	ὠφέλησα	ὠφέληκα	ὠφέλημαι	ὠφελήθην

Index of English Terms

Index of Greek Terms

NOTE: Some of the entries in this index include cross-references to English terms. These terms are listed in the Index of English Terms.

μάρτυς μάρτυρος ὁ, decl. of, 20
μέγας μεγάλη μέγα, decl. of, 6
μέν…δέ, with def. art., 99
μή + indicative, 76, 77; + imperative, 77;
    + opt. in fear and purpose clauses, 82; +
    participle, 90; + subju. 78–80
-μι verbs: aor. mid. participle, 16; forms
    (overview), 37–43; pres. act. participle,
    12; pres. mid.-pass. participle, 16. See also
    Athematic verbs; Irregular verbs

νεανίας –ου ὁ, decl. of, 19
νόσος –ου ἡ, decl. of, 19
νύξ νυκτός ἡ, decl. of, 20

ὁ ἡ τό, decl. of, 3. See also Definite article
ὅδε ἥδε τόδε, decl. of, 13. See also
    Demonstrative adjectives
οἶδα: forms, 45–46; introducing indirect
    statement with the participle, 92
ὅπως + fut. indic., 77; + opt., 82; + subju., 80
ὅς ἥ ὅ, decl. of, 4. See also Relative clauses;
    Relative pronouns
ὅστις ἥτις ὅτι/ὅ τι, decl. of, 4. See also
    Relative clauses; Relative pronouns
οὗ, decl. of, 3
οὐ μή + fut. indic., 77; + subju., 79
οὐδείς οὐδεμία οὐδέν, decl. of, 8
οὗτος αὕτη τοῦτο, decl. of, 6. See also
    Demonstrative adjectives

πᾶς πᾶσα πᾶν, decl. of, 9
Περικλῆς –έους ὁ, decl. of, 20
πόλις –εως ἡ, decl. of, 21
πολύς πολλή πολύ, decl. of, 6
πρέσβυς –εως ὁ, decl. of, 21

πρίν-clauses: acc. subject of, 56, 96; + inf.,
    95–96; + subju., 79; + opt., 82

σαφής –ές, decl. of, 8
σοφία –ας ἡ, decl. of, 19
σπονδή -ῆς ἡ, decl. of, 19
σύ, decl. of, 3
σφεῖς, decl. of, 3

τάλας –αινα –αν, decl. of, 9
τέτταρες –α, decl. of, 50
τίθημι, forms of, 37–43. See also -μι verbs
τις τι, decl. of, 8
τίς τί, decl. of, 8
τόλμα –ης ἡ, decl. of, 19
τρεῖς τρία, decl. of, 50
τριήρης –ους ἡ, decl. of, 20

ὑβριστής –οῦ ὁ, decl. of, 19
ὕδωρ –ατος τό, decl. of, 20
ὑμεῖς, decl. of, 3

φημί, forms, 45–46
φιλέω, forms, 45–46. See also Epsilon-
    contract verbs

χρή + acc. + inf., 56

ὤν οὖσα ὄν, decl. of, 11
ὡς + acc. person, 102; + adj. or adv. in
    exclamation, 101; + future participle, 102;
    + indic., 101; in indirect questions and
    statements, 102; + participle (non-future),
    102; + superlatives, 102
ὥστε, introducing result clause, with indic.
    or inf., 95

CPSIA information can be obtained
at www.ICGtesting.com
Printed in the USA
LVHW022127310719
626026LV00006B/27/P